cooking with

artisan

bread

cooking with
artisan
bread

Using rustic loaves
for perfect crostini, panini,
bruschetta, flavorful stuffings,
and inventive main courses

Gwenyth Bassetti and Jean Galton

SASQUATCH BOOKS
SEATTLE

Printed in the United States of America.
Distributed in Canada by Raincoast Books Ltd.
02 01 00 99   5 4 3 2

Cover design: Karen Schober
Cover photograph: Christopher Irion/The Image Bank
Interior design: Karen Schober
Illustrations: Laura Cook
Composition: Patrick David Barber Design
Copy editor: Susan Derecskey

Library of Congress Cataloging in Publication Data
Bassetti, Gwenyth.
    Cooking with artisan bread / Gwenyth Bassetti and Jean Galton.
        p.   cm.
    Includes index.
    ISBN 1-57061-135-1 (alk. paper)
    1. Cookery (Bread) 2. Bread. I. Galton, Jean. II. Title.
    TX769.B255 1998
    641.8'15—dc21   98-10123

Sasquatch Books
615 Second Avenue
Seattle, Washington 98104
(206) 467-4300
books@SasquatchBooks.com
http://www.SasquatchBooks.com

Sasquatch Books publishes high-quality adult nonfiction and children's books related to the Northwest (Alaska to San Francisco). For more information about our titles, contact us at the address above, or view our site on the World Wide Web.

*To the many bakers who through the years have made
Grand Central what it is today, who have taught me so much, and with
whom I keep learning the mysteries of bread.*
—G. B.

*This book is dedicated to my husband and best friend,
Ron Pellegrino, who was always ready to edit, taste, and help.*
—J. G.

Acknowledgments

*Our thanks to all the passionate and visionary bakers of the Northwest
for providing great stories and wonderful bread. And thanks to Gary Luke and
the staff at Sasquatch for pulling this book together.*

—The Authors

contents

contents

contents

A Revolution in Bread

*I remember how horrified we were at the sour, ashy-gray bread . . .
[Mrs. Shimerda] gave her family to eat. She mixed her dough, we discovered, in an old tin peck measure. . . . When she took the paste out
to bake she left smears of dough sticking to the sides of the measure
and let this residue ferment. The next time she made bread she scraped
this sour stuff down into the fresh dough to serve as yeast.*

—Willa Cather, *My Antonia*

Perhaps even before bread fell victim to prosperity and the surpluses of modern
agriculture, it succumbed to the pressures our immigrant forebears felt to assimi-
late. Faced with persistent disfavor toward all things foreign, the children of the
new Americans cast off their Old World culinary heritage as quickly as they did their
parents' language.

The rough dark loaf of Willa Cather's Bohemians might fit right into the array
of hand-formed, naturally leavened breads that are now the mark of our artisan
bakers, but it was looked upon with horror by their more established Nebraska
neighbors at the turn of the century. The frontier produced abundant wheat and
soon, affordable white flour. Within a generation, the American experience of our
pioneer forebears in the West became one of plenty and the possibility of having
to live "by bread alone" became remote.

The warm feelings homemade bread can evoke, along with lingering nostalgia
for those agrarian roots, has burst into our culture now and then, most curiously

perhaps in the bread machine phenomenon. Still it is clear that the emergence of the artisan baker and the ever-widening market for quality bread is the mark of something lasting, a genuine renaissance that is making a basic change in our eating habits. No area has provided more fertile ground for this reawakening than the Pacific Northwest. The birth rate for bakeries amounts to a population explosion, as good bread becomes common on our tables. We hope this little book will communicate the passion and commitment that goes into the loaf you buy and that these recipes will contribute to your enjoyment of every last crumb.

This rebirth of baking began in the eighties, but its roots reach back to the sixties and seventies when whole grains, handmade, and home grown were as much a part of the scene as peace symbols and rock music. Julia Child demystified French cooking with the publication of *Mastering the Art of French Cooking* and began a revolution of her own. Slowly, in pockets across the country, handmade cheeses, specialty coffees, better-than-ordinary wines, and something called "nouvelle cuisine" began to appear.

Artisan breads were next. Loaves made by hand, reflecting the centuries-old traditions of the European village baker, had flavor, texture, and aesthetic appeal; the baker's passion was an essential ingredient. Here was food that really could be the staff of life.

As with so many recent culinary trends, one of the sources of inspiration in America was Alice Waters's influential Chez Panisse restaurant in Berkeley, California. There, Steve Sullivan crafted wonderful breads that were baked in the restaurant's wood-fired oven. In the early eighties, Steve opened his acclaimed Acme Bakery in Berkeley, and at about the same time, Chuck Williams (of Williams-Sonoma fame) brought the Il Fornaio concept from Italy to Union Street in San Francisco. Within a very few years, the Bay Area had a handful of bakers making and selling crusty breads that were fermented slowly, shaped by hand, and baked in hearth ovens imported from Europe.

In 1986, in the midst of these early beginnings, Carol Field's now-classic book, *The Italian Baker*, was published. This definitive volume provided the first widely circulated information about the history and techniques of making regional Italian breads, with recipes that brought them into the realm of the possible for the home baker. Word was beginning to get out. The bread revolution was burgeoning and quite unknowingly the seeds of what would become Grand Central Bakery had been planted.

Years before, in 1972, I had joined two friends in opening a soup-and-sandwich restaurant in the newly renovated Grand Central Building in Seattle's Pioneer Square. Our concept was loosely defined but included making our own bread for the sandwiches. We called our little restaurant simply The Bakery. I took on the baking on the basis of a single summer's experience running a roadside stand with my children in the San Juan Islands, which advertised "Jam, Bread and Vegetables." Our lack of experience was exceeded only by our lack of money, and as our opening date approached we found ourselves offering a share in the business to our architect in lieu of his fee. The allure of the newly revitalized historic district and the novelty of our earthy approach fueled our early success and made it possible for us to learn by doing.

After four years I left The Bakery and Seattle for a new life on a farm, raising sheep and shallots in rural eastern Washington. My baking was once again focused on providing for family. The annual livestock show at the Cow Palace took us to San Francisco every fall and gave me the opportunity to discover the emerging bread scene first hand. My first effort to sample the fare at Acme Baking was thwarted by a SOLD OUT sign. I eventually did succeed, however, and came home thoroughly inspired. Back home, I employed a complex system involving spray bottles of water and bricks in my oven but didn't get very much further than simple sourdough. It wasn't until I got my hands on a copy of *The Italian Baker* that I began experimenting in earnest.

Widowed and with children grown, I began going back and forth to Seattle. In

1988 Alan Black, my longtime friend and landlord at The Bakery, purchased the restaurant. When Alan asked for an idea on how to update the concept of the operation, there was little doubt where my interest lay: bread. A couple of trips to San Francisco convinced us that starting such a bakery was possible. We found equipment and an inspired baker in Thomas Solis, who had the passion of a true artisan. He had baked for Joyce Goldstein at her Square One restaurant in San Francisco and when we met him his studio was a veritable bread laboratory. He agreed to come to Seattle for three months to help us get started. It was June 1989. The Bakery, now remodeled, was renamed the Grand Central Bakery. We were ready. Thomas was in Seattle and although the Italian hearth oven we had found was still in San Francisco, Thomas and I started developing recipes without it, baking our prototype loaves in the oven of a gas range. When the oven finally did arrive, we were ready to begin a modest production of about five varieties of what we called "rustic breads." We gave them mostly Italian names and started selling in our retail shop and to a few restaurants.

At about that time a young woman chef by the name of Leslie Mackie walked into the bakery, chatted with Thomas, left a resumé, and vanished. When I asked about her I was told, "Oh, she's gone back to Portland, I think . . ." But soon she reappeared and signed on to work with Thomas for his last month. She brought her great talent and an appetite whetted for bread. As our first head baker, she stayed with us through our crucial first four years before leaving to start her own successful Macrina Bakery.

In November of that first year, *The Seattle Times* headlined an article, "Run, Don't Loaf, to the Grand Central Bakery!" Longtime food editor John Hinterberger praised our Italian-style Como loaf, and lines formed the very next day. What was already a brisk demand became impossible to supply; we obviously needed additional space. We located 4500 square feet in Seattle's industrial area, bought a used French hearth oven, and started making more bread. Ten years later, the Grand

Central had seven locations in Portland and Seattle.

The Grand Central had grown at a giddy pace while, at the same time, similar bakeries who equaled or exceeded our volume emerged in both Portland and Seattle. As the established bakeries expanded, more new bakers and bakeries, committed to the principles of artisan baking, turned up in towns and villages from Gig Harbor, Washington, to Ketchum, Idaho. The growing appreciation of handcrafted bread and the bakers who provide it seems to mesh particularly well with Northwest values and to fit right in to this region's lifestyle. "Good bread saves a lot of cooking," we say. We hope you will find inspiration in these pages to use and appreciate every last crumb!

—Gwenyth Bassetti

In the Beginning,
There Was Bread

I began my cooking career as a teenager making bread. Not the type of artisan bread that has inspired this book, but the lumpy, soggy, and leaden loaves turned out by many a novice baker. Luckily for those who had to eat the stuff, I took a break from bread baking and began a concentrated effort to find the best loaves around. This exploration lead me to wonderful sourdoughs and baguettes with incredible crusts and springy crumbs. Artisan bread became a staple on my table.

Several years ago, when my husband and I moved to Seattle, one of my first crusades was to locate artisan bread. I found much more than I ever could have hoped for. After a tour of the local bakeries, I was amazed at the variety, quality, and quantity of handmade bread in the Northwest. Since then, I have occasionally been wistful for sunshine, but I have never been wanting for bread.

Since several loaves of artisan bread are usually residing in my kitchen, odd parts, ends, and chunks can frequently be found in the breadbox. This book is a result of a very serious commitment to waste nothing, especially when it comes to superb bread. By utilizing varieties of bread crumbs, croutons, irregular chunks, ends, and thick and thin slices, you can transform leftover bread into great starters, soups, sandwiches, main courses, breakfast and brunch dishes, and desserts. And should you be bitten by the baking bug, we've included a recipe for a homemade artisan-style bread and another one for pizza crust. Our hope is that this book will spare you the guilt of throwing away another wedge of slightly stale—but still wonderful—bread.

—Jean Galton

the
recipes

WHAT IS ARTISAN BREAD?

Artisan (är'ti-zen) n: a person manually skilled in making a particular product: a craftsperson.

As the Bread Revolution took shape a decade ago, so-called rustic, peasant, French, and Italian breads were linked not so much by their shape or ingredients or style as by the fact that they were watched over by an artisan—touched by hand, assessed by the eye, and subject to the baker's judgment at every step. The term *artisan* has come to stand for commitment to production methods that employ traditional skills distinct from the highly controlled and automated production systems of the factory bakery. The term has also come to imply breads made without stabilizers, dough conditioners, and preservatives. Even though consistent quality is always the goal in artisan bakeries and high standards are a given, artisan breads differ from day to day and from loaf to loaf. Variations of shape, color, and texture are testimony to the human touch that is the essence of these breads and to the organic nature of bread itself. As we naturally assess our first sip of a bottle of wine, so too might we make fine distinctions in our daily loaf.

Basic Country-Style Bread

It is not the intent of this book to focus on the process of creating artisan breads. However, because we believe that making bread is one of the simple pleasures of this life, we start with the following basic recipe for a country-style hearth loaf.

Makes two 6-inch round loaves

Slow fermentation, maximum hydration, and very little or no commercial yeast are the keys to the open-textured, crusty breads that reflect the traditions of the European countryside. The recipe that follows utilizes a starter—that is, a small amount of fermented dough made ahead of time—which serves as leavening. Although measuring by weight is more accurate than measuring by volume, this recipe gives amounts in cups and spoons (with flour also by weight), since few North Americans are equipped with kitchen scales.

Fermenting dough is a living organism and is adaptable and responsive to its environment. To mature well it needs time and attention, but the time schedule suggested is only a guide. You can slow down or speed up the process to fit your own schedule. After a few tries you will come up with your own plan of action. Just remember it is better to plan on extra time than to hurry the process. To make a loaf for Saturday night dinner, start on Thursday evening.

Equipment: Heavy-duty stand mixer, two 6-inch shallow baskets or bowls lined with dish towels, a pizza peel or rimless baking sheet, and oven tiles or a pizza stone.

STARTER: THURSDAY EVENING (15 MINUTES)

¼ teaspoon active dry yeast
1 cup water at room temperature (72° to 75°F)
2 cups unbleached all-purpose flour (10 ounces)

Dissolve the yeast in ¼ cup of the water. Let sit until frothy, about 10 minutes. Place the yeast mixture and the remaining ¾ cup water in the bowl of a heavy-duty mixer. Stir to mix. Add the flour and mix with the paddle until smooth, about 2 to 3 minutes. Scrape the mixture into a bowl large enough to allow for the starter to triple in size. Cover the bowl loosely with plastic wrap and let rise overnight at room temperature. (This starter makes enough for 2 batches of bread. You may freeze the excess or store it, covered, for 2 to 3 days in the refrigerator.)

DOUGH: FRIDAY MORNING (30 MINUTES)

¼ teaspoon active dry yeast
1½ cups water, room temperature (72° to 75°F)
1 cup starter
1 tablespoon olive oil (optional)
4 cups unbleached all-purpose flour (20 ounces)
2 teaspoons salt
Cornmeal, for dusting

Combine the yeast and water in the bowl of a heavy-duty mixer and mix with the paddle until combined. Add the starter and blend until smooth. Mix in the olive oil, if using, and half of the flour. Mix on low speed for 2 minutes. With a spatula, mix the salt into remaining flour. Switch from the paddle to the dough hook. Add the remaining flour and mix with the hook for 3 to 4 minutes. Scrape dough from the hook once or twice during mixing. The dough should come away cleanly from the sides of the bowl and take on a smooth, velvety look. Turn the dough onto a floured board and knead lightly. Place in a lightly oiled bowl, cover loosely, and let rise for 2 to 3 hours. Refrigerate until Saturday morning.

SHAPING AND FINAL RISE: SATURDAY MORNING (ABOUT 30 MINUTES)

Turn the dough out onto a floured board and cut in half. Cover the pieces with a kitchen towel and let rest for 30 minutes. Shape each piece into a ball, pinching the seams together to seal. Place each ball in a well-floured 6-inch basket or bowl lined with a towel, seam side up. Cover and let rise until nearly double, about 3 to 4 hours depending upon the room temperature.

SCORING AND BAKING: SATURDAY NOON (1 HOUR)

Line the oven rack with tiles or a pizza stone and preheat the oven to 450°F. Place an enamel or cast-iron frying pan in the bottom of a gas oven or on the lowest rack of an electric oven.

Turn the loaves over, seam side down, onto a peel or baking sheet without edges (baking sheet serves as a peel if you don't have one) dusted with cornmeal. With a very sharp knife or razor blade, score 3 to 4 cuts about ¼ inch deep on the diagonal across the top of the loaf. Carefully pour about 1 cup water into the hot frying pan and quickly close the oven door to trap the steam. After about 1 minute slide the loaves, one at a time, onto the stone. Turn the oven down to 400°F. Bake until a rich brown, about 40 minutes. The loaves will sound hollow when tapped on the bottom. Cool thoroughly before slicing.

Variations:

Add ½ cup (5 ounces) coarsely ground whole wheat flour or cornmeal, preferably stoneground.

Add ½ cup pitted kalamata olives.

To form rolls, divide the dough into 10 equal-size balls. Let rise 1 hour or until nearly double in size. Before baking, lightly score. Bake 30 to 35 minutes.

BREAD BASICS

Storing

Artisan breads by definition have no preservatives. Long fermentation helps extend the flavor life of the bread, and the firm crusts of hearth-baked breads hold the interior moisture. The first thing to go is the character of the crust. Moisture is the bread crust's worst enemy. For that reason, hearth breads are usually packaged in paper instead of plastic, as plastic traps the moisture and softens the crust. Serve bread the day you buy it if possible. For next-day use, place the loaf in a paper bag, then in a plastic bag, close tightly, and store in a cool, dark spot. Do not refrigerate, as modern refrigerators have fans and tend to dry the bread. For longer storage, freeze, wrapped as above. Frozen bread is best used within a couple of weeks.

Refreshing

To refresh bread that has been stored for one or two days, place the unwrapped loaf in a 400°F oven for 7 to 10 minutes. In an emergency, wrap a frozen loaf in foil and thaw in a moderate oven (325°F) for 15 to 20 minutes, depending on size of loaf. When thawed, unwrap the bread and turn up the heat to 400°F for an additional 5 to 7 minutes. The bread you buy today may have come from the oven yesterday evening, and by dinnertime it may have endured 24 hours of Northwest dampness. Even a fresh loaf can sometimes benefit from a quick refreshing prior to serving.

Slicing

Slice hearth breads for the table with an eye to the presentation. A good-quality bread knife with a serrated edge is essential. Cut a bâtard or round loaf in half the long way. Turn the loaf, cut side down, and cut it in half again. Slice each quarter to the desired thickness. Try not to slice all the way through so that the slices just hold together but can be easily pulled apart at the table. Cut baguettes slightly on the diagonal, also leaving a hinge that can easily be torn. If you don't have a long basket, cut the baguette in half and place it crisscrossed in a round or oval basket. Hearth-style breads are not usually sold sliced, but most bakeries will slice on request. A sliced loaf can be a convenience for sandwiches or for children not up to the bread knife. You might want to keep a sliced loaf in the freezer so you can take out a slice or two in an emergency.

Serving

Bread adds ceremony to mealtime. It is something to start eating before everyone is served and something to linger over as conversation extends the dinner hour. Good bread can stand alone, but if calories are not a concern, serve it with butter for spreading or olive oil for dipping.

Starters

Taramasalata

Makes ¾ cup

In Greece, this traditional dip would be part of an offering of meze, *or small appetizer dishes. It's usually a silken puree of salted mullet or cod roe, called* tarama, *and leftover bread. Look for bottled* tarama *at specialty stores in the refrigerated section. For a special treat, make this with golden whitefish roe from Flathead Lake in Montana. It is lighter in flavor than* tarama, *so reduce the amount of lemon juice to two tablespoons. Garnish the top with a sprinkling of roe.*

3 tablespoons minced Walla Walla or red onion
1 small clove garlic, minced
¼ cup tarama or golden whitefish roe (see Note)
3 tablespoons fresh lemon juice
3½ ounces country white or sourdough bread, crusts removed
   (about four ½-inch slices), torn into 1-inch pieces
¼ cup extra virgin olive oil
¼ cup canola oil
Large pinch of cayenne
Freshly ground black pepper, to taste
Olives, for garnish
Chunks of crusty bread for dipping

Combine the onion, garlic, tarama, and lemon juice in a food processor. Pour ½ cup water into a bowl and drop in 1 piece of bread at a time. As soon as the bread has soaked up the water, drop it into the feed tube of the food processor with the motor running. Continue with all the bread and pour in any remaining water. With the motor still running, drizzle in the olive oil and canola oil until well combined. Add the cayenne and black pepper and refrigerate for several hours to blend the flavors.

To serve, transfer to a bowl, garnish with olives, and serve with bread.

Note: Golden whitefish roe is available from Seattle Caviar Company, (206) 323-3005.

Middle Eastern Walnut and Pomegranate Spread

Makes 1 ¼ cups

This walnut spread, also from Grand Central's chef Pandora de Green, features pomegranate molasses. A thick concentrate of pomegranate juice, the molasses has a distinctive tangy flavor and aroma. It is available at Middle Eastern markets and by mail order.

> *1 cup walnut pieces*
> *1 red bell pepper, roasted, peeled, and seeded (see page 69)*
> *¼ cup chopped Italian flat-leaf parsley*
> *1 clove garlic, chopped*
> *1 jalapeño, seeded and chopped*
> *2 tablespoons olive oil*
> *1 ½ tablespoons fresh lemon juice*
> *1 tablespoon pomegranate molasses (see Note)*
> *1 teaspoon ground cumin*
> *1 teaspoon salt*
> *½ teaspoon freshly ground black pepper*
> *Pieces of flatbread or chunks of country white bread*

Preheat the oven to 350°F. Place the walnuts on a baking sheet and toast until lightly browned, about 10 minutes. Let cool.

Put the walnuts in a food processor. Cut the pepper flesh into chunks and put in the food processor with the nuts. Add the remaining ingredients except the bread. Process until pureed to a spreadable consistency (it will not become smooth).

Refrigerate and serve chilled or at room temperature with bread.

Note: Pomegranate molasses is available at Pacific Food Importers and The Souk (both in Seattle) or by mail order: Dean and DeLuca, 560 Broadway, New York, NY 10012, (800) 221-7714 or (212) 431-1691; Kalustyan, 123 Lexington Ave., New York, NY 10016, (212) 685-3416.

PITTING OLIVES

Need pitted olives for a recipe? Here's how. Take an olive and lay it on a cutting board. Holding the handle of the knife with one hand, place the widest part of the blade of your knife (a chef's knife or any knife with a wide blade, a cleaver, even a spatula will do) on top of the olive and press down hard with the other hand. The olive will split open, and you can easily remove the pit.

Mushroom Tapenade

Makes 2 cups

Tapenade, an olive, anchovy, and caper spread, is a specialty of Provence. Here, it is combined with dried and fresh mushrooms to deepen the flavors even further. Let the tapenade mellow for several hours or even a day before serving. If it has been refrigerated, make sure to bring it back to room temperature.

½ cup boiling water
½ ounce (about ½ cup) dried porcini mushrooms
⅓ cup plus 1 tablespoon extra virgin olive oil
3 to 4 medium cremini or button mushrooms, cleaned and
    thinly sliced (about 1 cup)
2 large cloves garlic, minced
1 cup (6 ounces) kalamata olives, pitted
1 cup (6 ounces) oil-cured black olives, pitted
10 anchovy fillets
1½ teaspoons fresh thyme leaves
2 tablespoons small capers, rinsed and drained
1 teaspoon freshly ground black pepper
Thinly sliced toasts or croûtes

Pour the boiling water over the dried mushrooms in a bowl. Let stand for 10 minutes. Drain and rinse the mushrooms, saving the soaking liquid for another dish, and coarsely chop. Set aside.

Heat the 1 tablespoon of oil in a large skillet over high heat. Add the fresh mushrooms and cook, turning once or twice, until browned, about 3 to 4 minutes. Add the garlic and dried mushrooms and stir for 30 seconds, or until the garlic is fragrant. Scrape the contents of the pan into a food processor and add the olives, anchovies, thyme, capers, and pepper. Process until smooth. With the motor running, pour in the ⅓ cup of olive oil. Scrape into a bowl or jar and let stand for at least several hours before serving. Serve with toasts or croûtes.

DIPPING OILS

Here are two different oils to use as appetizers or snacks. Cut some bread into thick wedges or chunks for dipping. For instructions for roasting peppers, see page 69.

Mixed Roasted Pepper Dipping Oil

Makes ½ cup

1 medium red pepper, roasted, peeled, and seeded
1 poblano chili, roasted, peeled, and seeded
1 jalapeño pepper, roasted, peeled, and seeded
½ cup extra virgin olive oil
1 teaspoon fresh thyme leaves
Pinch of salt

Dice the red pepper, poblano, and jalapeño and put in a food processor. Add the olive oil, thyme, and salt and process until smooth. Pour into a jar. Refrigerate for 1 day, then strain. Let come back to room temperature or reheat and use warm.

Roasted Garlic and Rosemary Dipping Oil

Makes ½ cup

1 head garlic, top 1 inch cut off
½ cup extra virgin olive oil
3 sprigs of rosemary
Pinch of salt

Preheat the oven to 350°F. Wrap the garlic in foil and bake until very soft, about 1 hour. Unwrap and let cool briefly. Squeeze out as much garlic as possible and scrape it into a saucepan. Add the olive oil, rosemary, and salt and bring to a simmer. Simmer until the rosemary starts to lose its bright green color, 1 to 2 minutes. Remove from the heat. Let stand for 1 hour. Strain and serve.

Grand Central's Spicy Hummus

Makes 2½ cups

This hummus recipe, created by chef Pandora de Green of the Grand Central Bakery's Cafe, has a healthy dose of cumin and cayenne. If you like extremely spicy food, use the entire amount of cayenne called for.

2 cups cooked dried chickpeas or 1 can (19 ounces) chickpeas,
    rinsed and drained, liquid reserved
3 tablespoons fresh lemon juice
2 tablespoons tahini
1 teaspoon ground cumin
1 teaspoon paprika
1 teaspoon salt
Pinch of freshly ground black pepper
¼ to ½ teaspoon cayenne
3 cloves garlic, coarsely chopped
1 tablespoon light sesame oil (not toasted)
¼ cup chickpea cooking liquid or water
Pieces of flatbread or chunks of country white, sourdough,
    or light whole wheat bread

Put all the ingredients except the chickpea liquid and bread in a food processor and puree until well combined, scraping down the bowl several times. Add the liquid and puree until silky smooth. Refrigerate and serve chilled or at room temperature, with bread.

BRUSCHETTA, CROSTINI, AND CROÛTES

Bruschetta, crostini, and croûtes: different names for the same thing? Not quite.

Bruschetta is a thick slice of grilled bread, usually rubbed with garlic, drizzled with olive oil, and sprinkled with coarse salt. Bruschette (plural for bruschetta), with a variety of toppings, can serve as a first course or the centerpiece of a light lunch.

Crostini, on the other hand, are much thinner slices that are toasted rather than grilled. Though they too are sometimes topped, they are usually served alongside spreads and various antipasti.

Croûtes, from the French rather than the Italian tradition, are thin toasts, similar to crostini.

Bruschetta with Wild Mushrooms and Herbs

Serves 4

Since the Northwest is blessed with such a huge variety of wild mushrooms, making a mushroom bruschetta couldn't be easier. Use whatever is in season or a combination of wild and cultivated mushrooms. Just make sure the bread can stand up to the topping. It's got to be flavorful, thick, and crusty and rubbed generously with garlic and olive oil.

¼ cup extra virgin olive oil
1 pound mixed fresh mushrooms such as chanterelles, morels,
  oyster, porcini, shiitake, or button, cleaned and
  cut into bite-size pieces
½ teaspoon salt
½ tablespoon chopped fresh rosemary leaves
½ tablespoon chopped fresh sage leaves
2 tablespoons chopped Italian flat-leaf parsley
¼ teaspoon grated lemon zest
½ teaspoon freshly ground black pepper
4 thick (¾-inch) slices country white, sourdough, or light
  whole wheat bread
2 large cloves garlic, cut in half
¼ cup shredded asiago

Preheat the grill or broiler. Heat 2 tablespoons of the olive oil in a large skillet. Over high heat, add the mushrooms and salt and cook, stirring frequently, until the mushrooms are soft and the liquid has evaporated, 4 to 5 minutes. Stir in the herbs, lemon zest, and pepper. Set aside.

Grill or broil the bread until golden on both sides, about 2 minutes per side. Brush with the remaining olive oil and rub vigorously with the cut sides of the garlic. Place the bread on a platter and divide the mushrooms evenly on the bread. Sprinkle with the asiago. Serve immediately.

Crostini with Chicken Livers and Caramelized Onions

Serves 8 as a first course

Crostini are the perfect underpinnings for this savory topping. When Washington State Walla Wallas are in season (not long compared to standard yellow onions), combine them with sautéed chicken livers and Parmesan cheese for a perfect first course.

> 24 thin (½-inch) slices baguette
> ¼ cup extra virgin olive oil
> 1 large (about 1 pound) Walla Walla or other sweet onion,
>   cut in half lengthwise and thinly sliced
> 1 teaspoon sugar
> 1 pound chicken livers, rinsed and cut in half if large
> 1½ teaspoons fresh chopped thyme leaves or ½ teaspoon dried
>   thyme, crumbled
> ½ teaspoon salt
> ½ teaspoon freshly ground black pepper
> ½ cup Parmesan shavings
> Chopped Italian flat-leaf parsley, for garnish

Preheat the oven to 400°F. Brush both sides of the bread slices with 2 tablespoons of the olive oil and spread on a baking sheet. Bake until lightly golden on both sides but not hard, about 8 minutes. Set aside.

Meanwhile, heat 1 tablespoon of the olive oil in a large skillet over medium-high heat. Add the onion and sugar and cook, stirring frequently, until the onion is very soft and sweet, about 20 minutes. Remove from the pan and keep warm.

In the same pan, heat the remaining 1 tablespoon olive oil over high heat. Add the livers, thyme, salt, and pepper and sauté, stirring frequently, until just cooked through, 3 to 4 minutes.

To serve, spoon about 1 teaspoon onions onto each crostini and top with a chicken liver and a shaving of Parmesan. Sprinkle with parsley and serve. To serve a crowd, place the livers in a bowl and sprinkle with the parsley. Place the onions and Parmesan in separate bowls and pile the crostini on a platter to let people help themselves.

LA PANZANELLA

Seattle, Washington

At La Panzanella, philosophy is as indispensable as a good oven. The three guiding principles are: *l'occhio*, the eye that watches the bread's ever-changing variables; *la mano*, the hand that forms and tests each loaf; and *il cuore*, the heart that is the wellspring of the baker's passion for bread and life. La Panzanella's chief philosopher and baker, Ciro Pasciutto, along with his co-owner and wife, Kim, relies on these fundamentals to shape and guide his daily commitment to producing fine rustic loaves.

After emigrating from Gaeta, Italy, in 1986, Ciro found Seattle's bread scene dismal. He began at once making bread for family and friends. Word spread. When friends opened Buongusto restaurant, they asked Ciro to make its bread; La Panzanella was born. As Seattle's appetite for all things Italian grew, so did La Panzanella.

Unlike most artisan bakeries in the Northwest, La Panzanella produces only one type of dough, a combination of unbleached white and whole wheat flours, water, salt, and a minute amount of yeast. The bread that results is a hearty, rustic Italian loaf, typical of breads found all along the Appian Way from Rome to Apulia. This same dough is formed into rolls, breadsticks, focaccia, and crackers, which are marketed to restaurants, hotels, caterers, wine shops, and specialty and small food stores. The breads are also sold at La Panzanella's new retail store, along with a small selection of regional *dolci*, or small pastries.

Using only one dough frees Ciro to lavish enthusiastic and loving attention on this only child, thus striking a balance between bread making as both an art and a business. It's his way of re-creating a village baker in the midst of a large metropolitan city.

Ciro's Panzanella

Serves 2

In panzanella, two humble ingredients, stale bread and ripe tomatoes, turn into a sublime salad. Of course, adding fresh basil, scallions, and the best extra virgin olive oil counts for something too. This recipe comes from Ciro Pasciutto of La Panzanella in Seattle.

4 ripe plum tomatoes, cored and thinly sliced crosswise
¼ teaspoon salt, or to taste
2 scallions, thinly sliced
1 Anaheim chili, seeded and chopped
10 fresh basil leaves, cut into chiffonade
2 tablespoons extra virgin olive oil
One 2-day-old loaf rustic bread, thinly sliced
Basil leaves, for garnish

Mix the tomatoes and salt in a small bowl. Let stand for 10 minutes.

Stir in 1 tablespoon water, the scallions, chili, basil, and olive oil. Stir to mix. Let stand for 1 hour. Taste for seasoning.

Place half the bread on a large plate. Top with half the tomato mixture and juices. Top with the remaining bread and tomato mixture. Garnish with additional basil.

Note: For a bit of heat, substitute one seeded and chopped jalapeño for the Anaheim chili.

Marcella Rosene's Endive Leaves Stuffed with Red Bread

Makes 48 appetizers

This winning finger food is from Marcella Rosene of Pasta & Co., Seattle's premier retailer of take-out foods and specialty groceries. The bread stuffing is turned red by a good soak in red wine vinegar and marinara sauce. This recipe is from her 1997 cookbook, Pasta & Co. Encore.

10 ounces day-old country white bread, crusts removed, and torn
   into ½-inch pieces (5 cups)
¼ to ⅓ cup red wine vinegar
⅔ cup homemade or best-quality bottled marinara sauce
   (see Note)
⅓ cup extra virgin olive oil
1½ tablespoons finely minced garlic
¼ teaspoon salt
Freshly ground black pepper, to taste
¼ cup capers, rinsed and drained
¼ cup finely chopped Italian flat-leaf parsley
6 or 7 heads Belgian endive
Finely chopped parsley or chives, for garnish
Extra virgin olive oil, for drizzling (optional)

Put the bread in a bowl and toss with enough vinegar to cover. Let stand for 10 to 15 minutes, or until soft. Stir in the marinara sauce with a fork, and add the olive oil, garlic, salt, and pepper. Work well with a fork or process quickly in a food processor to make a coarse paste. Do not puree. Remove from the processor and fold in the capers and parsley. Refrigerate until ready to use.

To serve, cut the endive heads about 1 inch above the root end and separate the leaves. Fill each leaf with about 2 teaspoons of the bread mixture. Arrange the filled leaves on a serving dish. Just before serving, garnish with parsley or chives and drizzle with olive oil, if desired.

Note: Pasta & Co. bottles their own marinara sauce. It is available by mail order from Pasta & Co., 1318 E. Pine St., Seattle, WA 98122, (206) 322-1644, http://www.pastaco.com.

AMERICAN FLOUR VERSUS EUROPEAN

For a long time, conventional wisdom had it that the reason we couldn't get good French bread in North America was that the flour in Europe was better. Not so. In fact, European bakers prize North American wheat, which is higher in protein and of a superior quality than wheat grown in European fields that have been tilled for centuries. So what is the difference? American bakers do find differences in the baking qualities of French flour when compared to generally available home-grown flours, but they have now proven to themselves that the master baker can adapt to these differences, even using the differences to their advantage. Classic European-style breads of high quality can be made with flours from either side of the Atlantic. The long absence of good bread in the United States had more to do with losing the art of baking than anything else.

Megan Bassetti's Favorite Caesar Salad

Serves 8 to 10

Hand-cut garlic croutons set Megan Bassetti's (Gwen's stepdaughter) caesar salad apart from the crowd. Anchovy lovers may want to add very thin anchovy fillets. If you are concerned about salmonella, eliminate the eggs from the recipe, since coddling will not eliminate the risk.

1¼ cups extra virgin olive oil
Juice of 1 lemon
¼ cup seasoned rice vinegar
2 cloves garlic, run through a garlic press
1 tablespoon sugar
Salt and freshly ground black pepper, to taste
1 tablespoon anchovy paste
3 tablespoons unsalted butter
6 thick (¾-inch) slices Como bread or other country
    white bread, cut into cubes
2 heads romaine lettuce
2 large eggs, at room temperature (optional)
½ cup grated Parmesan

Combine 1 cup of the oil, the lemon juice, vinegar, 1 clove of the garlic, the sugar, salt, pepper, and anchovy paste in a blender or food processor. Blend or process for 30 to 40 seconds or until smooth. Set aside.

Melt the butter and the remaining ¼ cup olive oil together in a large frying pan over medium-low heat. Add the remaining clove of garlic and toss in the bread. Cook, stirring frequently, until the bread is crisp and brown, about 15 minutes. Cool slightly.

Meanwhile, bring a small pot of water to a boil. Add the eggs, if using, and simmer for 90 seconds to coddle the egg. Drain and rinse under cold water to stop the cooking.

Chop the romaine into 1-inch-wide pieces and place in a large salad bowl. Break the eggs over the lettuce and add the croutons, dressing, and Parmesan. Toss well. Taste and season with more salt and black pepper if necessary.

ORGANIC BAKING

Many artisan bakers are sympathetic to the environmentally responsible principles of organic farming as well as the healthy aspects of chemical-free food. Flour that carries the label Certified Organically Grown has passed rigorous inspections all along the road from farmer to miller to baker. The bakery that in turn markets organic products must have proven to a local certifying organization that that every ingredient used carries such a label.

Organic flour costs substantially more than non-organic flour because of actual increased costs of production and lower average yields per acre. Though the market for organic wheat is increasing, it still represents a very small percentage of the total market and thus benefits little from the economies of scale.

The Essential Baking Company in Seattle and the Black Bear Bakery in Portland are the major Certified Organic bakeries in the Northwest. Essential Baking, begun in 1994, led the way. The founding "gang of five" as they call themselves, led by Jeff Fairhall and head baker George DePasquale, now employ one hundred people and send more than four thousand loaves of bread to Puget Sound markets and area restaurants every day. Located in Seattle's Fremont district, Essential Baking sells wholesale only, but they look forward to adding a retail outlet in the near future. Launched in 1997 by the Grand Central Bakery, the Black Bear label provides an organic choice in Portland's expanding marketplace.

Fried Eggplant Sticks

Serves 4

Keep some homemade, dried bread crumbs on hand for this wonderful eggplant appetizer. Somehow, frying eggplant transforms it to become creamy and delicate inside, surrounded by a golden brown, crunchy shell. Serve with lemon wedges or lemon mayonnaise (lemon juice, zest, and chopped cilantro stirred into prepared mayonnaise) for a great hors d'oeuvre.

> 1 large (1 to 1¼ pounds) eggplant, cut lengthwise into
>   ½-inch slices, then into ½-inch-wide sticks
> 1 teaspoon salt
> 2 teaspoons ground cumin
> ½ teaspoon cayenne
> ½ cup all-purpose flour
> 3 large eggs
> 1¼ cups fine dry bread crumbs
> Olive oil, for frying

Sprinkle the eggplant with the salt, put in a colander, and place a large plate over the eggplant. Weight the plate down with a large can or a pot filled with water and place the colander in a large bowl or in the sink. Let stand for 1 hour.

Mix the cumin and cayenne with the flour and put in a shallow bowl or pie plate. Put the eggs in another shallow bowl pie plate and lightly beat with 1 tablespoon water. Put the bread crumbs in another. Working in batches, lightly dredge the eggplant in the flour, shaking off the excess. Dip the eggplant in the eggs. Remove, letting the excess drip off, then dredge in the bread crumbs. Place on a rack or wax paper while coating all the rest.

Heat ½ inch olive oil in a large heavy skillet over medium-high heat until a cube of bread browns in 40 seconds. Place several of the eggplant sticks in the oil, making sure not to crowd the pan. Fry, turning once or twice, until golden, 2 to 3 minutes. Drain on toweling. Repeat with the remaining eggplant. Serve hot.

Soups

Pappa al Pomodoro

Serves 6

This traditional tomato and bread soup from Italy depends on flavorful tomatoes, rich extra virgin olive oil, and great rustic bread for success. Since fresh tomatoes aren't always optimal, we like to use Muir Glen Organic canned tomatoes (from California).

¼ cup plus 2 tablespoons extra virgin olive oil

3 large cloves garlic, coarsely chopped

Pinch of crushed red pepper

2 cans (28 ounces each) tomatoes, drained (with juice reserved)
    and chopped

8 ounces (about 6 cups) country white or sourdough bread,
    cut into 1-inch chunks

1 cup Chicken Broth (page 57)

1 teaspoon salt

½ teaspoon freshly ground black pepper

¼ cup coarsely chopped fresh basil leaves

¼ cup chopped Italian flat-leaf parsley

1 teaspoon chopped fresh thyme

Heat ¼ cup of the olive oil in a large pot over medium-high heat. Add the garlic and red pepper and cook 30 seconds, or until the garlic is fragrant and turning golden. Add the tomatoes, bread, 2 cups of the reserved juices, and the broth and bring to a boil. Reduce the heat and simmer until thickened and the tomatoes have broken down, about 30 minutes. Stir in the salt, pepper, basil, parsley, thyme, and remaining 2 tablespoons olive oil. Let stand for 1 hour. Serve at room temperature.

Walla Walla Onion Soup

Serves 6

This French-inspired onion soup is especially sweet and creamy when made with Walla Walla onions. These juicy, mild onions are available only from June to September, though Maui or Vidalia onions can be substituted.

> 2 tablespoons unsalted butter
> 1 tablespoon canola oil
> 6 large Walla Walla or other sweet onions, cut in half and
>   thinly sliced (about 4 to 5 pounds)
> 1 teaspoon sugar
> 2 tablespoons all-purpose flour
> 2 bay leaves
> 1 cup dry white wine
> 4 cups Chicken Broth (page 57) or low-sodium canned broth
> Salt and freshly ground black pepper, to taste
> Pinch of cayenne
> 6 thick (¾-inch) slices baguette
> 2 cups grated Gruyère, Jarlsberg, or Swiss cheese (8 ounces)

Heat the butter and oil in a large soup pot over medium-high heat. Add the onions and sugar and cook, stirring occasionally, until the onions are light brown and very tender, about 40 minutes.

Stir in the flour and cook for 1 minute. Add the bay leaves and wine and simmer until the wine is slightly reduced, about 2 minutes. Stir in the broth and bring to a boil. Reduce the heat and simmer 20 minutes. Remove and discard the bay leaves. Season with salt and pepper.

Preheat the broiler. Toast the baguette slices and top each with cheese, dividing evenly. Broil until melted and bubbling, 1 to 2 minutes. Place one in each of 6 warm soup bowls. Ladle the soup over the bread and serve.

Minestrone and Ribollita

Serves 6 to 8

Thickened with country bread and reheated, today's minestrone becomes transformed into tomorrow's ribollita. Literally meaning re-boiled, ribollita finds a place on many contemporary Italian menus, but it originated in the country kitchens of Tuscany. The wild herbs that scent the countryside were traditionally used to enhance minestrone, a simple soup of garden vegetables. For Gwen Bassetti's version, you can use herbs straight from your garden.

1½ cups dried white beans, rinsed and picked over

Salt, to taste

6 tablespoons extra virgin olive oil

1 small Walla Walla or other sweet onion, thinly sliced

3 stalks celery, including leaves, coarsely chopped

3 medium carrots, thinly sliced

2 thin slices lean salt pork or thick-sliced bacon

5 small Yukon Gold or Yellow Finn potatoes, scrubbed
    and cut into ½-inch cubes (about 8 ounces)

2 medium leeks, white and light green parts only, washed
    well and thinly sliced

3 to 4 cups Chicken Broth (page 57) or beef stock,
    preferably homemade

2 tablespoons tomato paste or ½ cup marinara sauce

3 fresh or canned plum tomatoes, peeled, seeded, and diced

½ medium savoy cabbage, cored and finely shredded (about
    4 cups)

¼ teaspoon crushed red pepper

¼ cup chopped Italian flat-leaf parsley

¼ cup chopped fresh basil

3 cloves garlic, crushed with the flat of a knife

6 sprigs of thyme

6 to 8 thin (½-inch) slices day-old country white bread

Extra virgin olive oil, for drizzling
Chopped Italian flat-leaf parsley and freshly grated
Parmesan, for garnish

Soak the beans in cold water to cover by about 3 inches for 12 hours or overnight, or place in a 2-quart saucepan with water to cover, bring to a boil, cover, remove from the heat, and let stand for 1 hour.

Drain the beans, return to the pot, and cover with 4 cups cold water. Bring to a boil, reduce the heat, and simmer until tender, about 30 to 45 minutes. Remove from the heat and add salt. Let the beans cool in the pot and reserve both the beans and the cooking liquid. (The beans may be prepared a day ahead.)

Heat 4 tablespoons of the olive oil in a heavy-bottomed fireproof 5- to 6-quart casserole or Dutch oven over medium-high heat. Add the onion, celery, and carrots and cook until soft, 8 to 10 minutes. Push to the side and add the salt pork or bacon and cook, stirring frequently, until browned, about 8 minutes. Add the potatoes, leeks, and 2 cups of the broth and simmer for 10 minutes, or until the potatoes are tender. Add the beans and reserved cooking liquid, the tomato paste, tomatoes, cabbage, red pepper, parsley, basil, and garlic. With a piece of cotton string or cheesecloth, tie the sprigs of thyme together and add to the pot. Simmer very gently, adding more broth as necessary, for about 40 minutes, or until the vegetables are very tender and soup is quite thick. Taste for seasoning. Remove and discard the bacon and thyme.

FOR MINESTRONE:

Grill or toast the bread and brush with the remaining 2 tablespoons olive oil. Place a bread slice in the bottom of a heated soup bowl and ladle the soup over. Drizzle with olive oil and sprinkle with parsley and Parmesan. Repeat with the remaining portions.

FOR RIBOLLITA:

Coarsely cut or tear up the bread and stir into the soup. Let cool, cover, and refrigerate. When ready to serve, place over medium-low heat and carefully add additional broth as necessary (the soup is very thick and will tend to stick to the bottom if you are not careful). Or, reheat the soup in a 300°F oven. Taste for seasoning. Serve in warm soup bowls, drizzled with olive oil, and sprinkled with parsley and Parmesan.

Portuguese Garlic and Bread Soup

Serves 6

This spicy soup is redolent of cooked and chopped raw garlic. Traditionally, it's made simply with water instead of broth, but that seems a bit foreign to American palates. Make this when you have a cold or on one of those drippy gray winter days and you'll feel better very immediately.

20 cloves garlic, peeled and smashed with the flat of a knife
8 cups vegetable broth or Chicken Broth (page 57)
1 cup cilantro leaves and stems
2 teaspoons coarse salt
¼ cup fruity olive oil
6 thick (¾-inch) slices day-old country white, sourdough, light whole wheat bread, or yeasted cornbread
6 large eggs, cold
Freshly ground black pepper and chopped cilantro, for garnish
Olive oil, for drizzling

Combine 15 cloves of garlic in a large saucepan and the broth over medium-high heat and bring to a boil. Reduce the heat and simmer for 20 minutes. Strain and return to the pot.

Meanwhile, coarsely chop the remaining 5 cloves of garlic. In a food processor or with a mortar and pestle, pound the garlic, cilantro, and salt until a paste forms. Stir in the olive oil. Set aside.

Toast the bread in a toaster or broiler and cut into ¾-inch strips.

Bring the garlic broth just to a simmer. Break the eggs, one at a time, into a cup and slide into the broth. Poach for 2 minutes, then transfer to paper towels with a slotted spoon.

To serve, divide the cilantro puree among 6 soup bowls. Place the bread on top and pour in the garlic broth. Top each with a poached egg, sprinkle with pepper and cilantro, and drizzle with olive oil. Serve immediately.

Lentil-Mushroom Soup

Serves 6

Washington State is one of the country's premier growers of lentils. In this soup, brown or green lentils are combined with woodland mushrooms and Walla Walla onions, two other local products, and cooked until tender and nutty.

1 cup boiling water
1 ounce dried porcini mushrooms (about 1 cup)
¼ cup extra virgin olive oil
1 Walla Walla or other sweet onion, chopped
4 ounces chanterelles, cremini, or button mushrooms, cleaned
   and thinly sliced
3 cloves garlic, minced
2 imported bay leaves
8 sprigs of fresh thyme or 1 teaspoon dried thyme
1 cup dry white wine
1 cup brown or green lentils, rinsed and picked over
½ cup orzo or other small pasta
Salt and freshly ground black pepper, to taste
¼ cup chopped Italian flat-leaf parsley
6 thick (¾-inch) slices sourdough, country white, or light
   whole wheat bread
1 clove garlic, peeled and cut in half
Extra virgin olive oil, for drizzling

Pour the boiling water over the dried mushrooms in a bowl. Let stand for 10 minutes. Drain the mushrooms, reserving the mushroom soaking liquid, and coarsely chop, then set aside. Filter the soaking liquid through a coffee filter or double layer of paper towels. Set aside.

Heat 2 tablespoons of the olive oil in a large saucepan over medium-high heat. Add the onion and fresh mushrooms and cook, stirring frequently, until soft, 3 to 4 minutes. Stir in the garlic, bay leaves, and thyme and stir until the garlic is fragrant, about 1 minute. Stir in the dried mushrooms and the wine.

Add mushroom soaking liquid and bring to a boil. Simmer until the liquid is slightly reduced, about 5 minutes. Stir in the lentils and 7 cups water. Simmer until the lentils are soft, about 25 to 30 minutes. Stir in the pasta and cook until done, about 4 to 5 minutes. Remove the bay leaves and thyme sprigs and season with salt and pepper. Stir in the parsley.

Meanwhile, toast the bread either under the broiler or in a toaster, until lightly golden. Rub with the garlic and brush with some of the remaining 2 tablespoons olive oil. Place a slice in each of 6 soup bowls and ladle soup over the bread. Drizzle with additional olive oil and serve.

PEARL BAKERY

Portland, Oregon

Taking its name from the Pearl District in northwest Portland where designers and condos now dot a once exclusively industrial neighborhood, the Pearl Bakery opened its doors in 1997 and quickly became a focal point of the revitalized district. The sophisticated retail area is in front of a spacious production facility that puts out some of the best bread and pastries in town. Owner and founder Greg Mistell is one of the industry pioneers, a twenty-year veteran who admits to still finding it a challenge to make a good baguette. As a principal of Delfina's, an established wholesale bakery in Portland, Greg introduced quality bread to the Portland area. This latest venture reflects his broad experience and professional expertise—in both the quality of the product and the well-designed facility. Specialties like the fig bars with a touch of cumin share the spotlight with such breads as an open-textured ciabatta and a pain au levain.

NAMING THE BREADS

Names for traditional European breads are as varied as the places they come from and as diverse as the imaginations of their bakers. French breads are generally known by their shape, perhaps because the ingredients for bread were often controlled by law and therefore assumed to be uniform: baguette, or stick, thus the familiar long shape; *boule*, or ball; and that shape that is neither round nor long, the French, in their inimitable way, dubbed a bâtard—literally, bastard.

Reflecting the history of Italy itself, breads from that country often retain a distinct regional character with regional names. Salt was historically scarce and expensive around Florence, thus Tuscan bread is a loaf made with little or no salt. Pugliese is a name for breads that share the rustic character and round shape of legendary breads from Apulia, at the heel of Italy. Como, from Lake Como, suggests a link to traditional northern Italian breads. Ciabatta, another familiar export, originates in the north but is known rather for its unassuming look, that of an old slipper.

Our own traditions are still young and often derivative. While French names for shapes persist, Northwest artisan bakers are breaking away from the European regional references. Names like Yukon Gold potato loaf, Columbia, and Palouse now identify many local breads and may, at some future time, become legends themselves.

Chicken Broth

Makes about 8 cups

The difference between a good soup and an extraordinary one can often be related to the broth within. As good as canned broths can be, nothing beats the homemade variety.

2 to 3 pounds chicken wings or backs
3 quarts cold water
1 yellow onion, thinly sliced
1 leafy rib celery, thinly sliced
1 large carrot, thinly sliced
2 cloves garlic, thinly sliced
1 imported bay leaf
1 sprig flat-leaf Italian parsley
1 teaspoon salt, or to taste

Place the chicken and water in a large stockpot. Bring to boil over high heat. Skim off any foam that floats to the surface. Add onion, celery, carrot, garlic, bay leaf, parsley, and salt. Reduce heat and simmer broth, uncovered, over medium-low heat for 3 hours or until reduced by one third.

Set a fine strainer over a large bowl and pour broth into strainer. Discard solids. Fill sink halfway with ice water and place bowl carefully into sink to chill. When broth has chilled to at least room temperature, cover with plastic wrap and chill overnight.

Next day, lift the solid fat from the surface and discard. Ladle the broth into 1- or 2-cup containers and refrigerate or freeze. Broth will keep 2 to 3 days in the refrigerator or up to 4 months in the freezer.

MAKING BREAD CRUMBS, CROUTONS, AND CROÛTES

Bread Crumbs

It's economical, easy, and convenient to make and store bread crumbs. They are called for in recipes, but you'll also find that if you have them in your pantry, you'll use them in an impromptu way to top off a baked dish, to bulk up a filling, or to coat foods for frying.

For fresh crumbs: Remove heavy crusts, roughly cut the bread into cubes, and pulverize them in a food processor or blender. Do not to use bread that is too stale, as the staleness will come through. Store fresh bread crumbs in the freezer, double-bagged or in a puncture-proof container to avoid accidents. Experiment with different kinds of bread for a variety of flavors.

For dry crumbs: Slice the bread and dry it out on a baking sheet in a slow oven (250°F). Break up the bread and pulverize it in a food processor or blender, or crush with a rolling pin between two sheets of wax paper. Store dry bread crumbs in an airtight container. They keep quite well. If you are making a large quantity, freeze some for longer storage.

Croutons and Croûtes

All croutons are not alike. The shape and size affect the texture of a dish, the way the crouton absorbs flavors, and can provide unique visual interest as well. Croutons are cubes which can be cut larger or smaller depending on the desired effect. Torn croutons are an interesting variation, and they provide additional surface for absorption. They are particularly good for stuffing. To make croutons, remove heavy crusts from the bread and cut slices as thick as you want the cubes to be. Cut into cubes. For torn croutons, do not cut, but tear the bread into pieces. Croûtes are larger toasts for soups or to use as a base for canapés. They may be rounds cut from a baguette or slices from larger loaves cut into rounds, diamonds, or triangles.

For dry croutons: Toast the croutons in a 350°F oven until golden, stirring once or twice. Remove from the oven and toss with dried herbs and/or salt and pepper, if desired. Store the croutons in an airtight container.

For seasoned croutons: Toss the croutons in a large bowl with good-quality olive oil and such seasonings as garlic, mixed dried herbs, or crushed red pepper. Spread on a baking sheet and brown in a 350°F oven or sauté in a large pan, turning frequently. Toss with Parmesan cheese while they are still warm, if desired. Cool thoroughly and store in an airtight container. Be sure to check that they smell fresh before using.

For croûtes: Cut bread into slices ¾ to 1 inch thick. Use a cookie cutter to cut shapes if desired. Place the slices in a single layer on a baking sheet and bake slowly (300°F) until they are thoroughly dried out and lightly browned. Halfway through baking, you may want to brush with olive oil or melted butter. Croûtes can be made ahead of time and reheated before serving.

Pizza and Sandwiches

Cafe Lago's Pizza with
Heirloom Tomatoes and Ricotta Salata

Makes six 8-inch pizzas

Cafe Lago is a Seattle restaurant institution famous for its wood-fired pizza oven. Fueled by a variety of woods, this oven fires up to 800° or 900°F, turning out pizza with a crisp crust and a hint of wood smoke. Toppings vary seasonally—this one is a summer specialty. Heirloom tomatoes deliver incredible flavor and color; to slice the tomatoes thin enough, use a serrated knife. Ricotta salata, a salted and aged ewe's milk cheese from Italy, adds a tangy jolt. The pizza is finished off with a sprinkling of fresh basil, crumbled Greek oregano for a distinct Mediterranean flavor, and a drizzle of the finest extra virgin olive oil.

> *Classic Italian Pizza Dough (recipe follows)*
> *3 tablespoons extra virgin olive oil plus more for drizzling*
> *5 large cloves garlic, finely chopped*
> *4 to 5 ripe tomatoes, preferably mixed red and yellow*
> *   heirloom varieties, very thinly sliced*
> *2 cups crumbled ricotta salata, at room temperature*
> *Dried Greek oregano (see Note)*
> *8 large fresh basil leaves, cut into chiffonade*

Place a pizza stone in the oven and preheat to 550°F, or as high as your oven will go, for 30 minutes.

Gently flatten a dough ball on a floured board and begin stretching into a rough circle about 8 inches in diameter. Do not pound or pinch the dough or it will not stretch. Place the dough on a well-floured pizza peel or back of a baking sheet. Brush with olive oil and sprinkle with some of the garlic. Leaving a ½-inch rim, cover the dough with one sixth of the tomatoes, alternating red and yellow slices. Place on the stone and bake until the crust is light brown, about 3 to 4 minutes. While the pizza is baking, prepare the next round of dough. When the crust is browned, slide out the oven rack and sprinkle with about ⅓ cup of the ricotta salata. Slide the rack back in and bake 2 to 3 minutes longer, or until the cheese is slightly melted and the crust is browned.

Transfer to a plate and top with a pinch of oregano, a sprinkling of basil, and a drizzle of olive oil. Repeat with all the remaining dough balls. Serve hot.

Note: Greek oregano is available at Middle Eastern and specialty stores.

Classic Italian Pizza Dough

Makes six 8-inch pizza crusts

> 2 cups lukewarm water (72° to 75°F)
> 1½ teaspoons active dry yeast
> 7 to 8 cups unbleached all-purpose flour
> ½ tablespoon salt
> Olive oil

Combine ¼ cup of the water and the yeast in a large mixing bowl or heavy-duty mixer fitted with a paddle. Stir to dissolve the yeast. In another bowl, mix together 6 cups of the flour and the salt. Add 1 cup of the flour to the yeast mixture and mix with a wooden spoon or on low speed in mixer. Stir in the remaining water and start adding the flour, 1 cup at a time, mixing until smooth after each addition. Turn the flour out onto a well-floured board and knead, or change to dough hook on mixer and knead on medium speed, adding enough flour to make a soft but not wet dough. Knead until smooth and uniform, at least 5 minutes.

Divide the dough equally into 6 pieces and form into balls. Flatten with the palm of your hand. Place on a well-floured baking sheet, 3 to 4 inches apart. Brush the dough with olive oil and cover with plastic wrap. Let rise in a warm place for 2½ to 3 hours, or until doubled.

Layered Salmon Sandwich

Serves 4 to 6

This delicious sandwich puts a Northwest spin on the traditional Provençal pan bagna, which is typically a salade niçoise on bread. Here, grilled salmon substitutes for tuna and a rustic country loaf sits in for the baguettes. Feel free to play with the ingredients, substituting other greens (watercress, curly endive, or spinach), or adding cucumbers, tomatoes, and olives.

> ¾ pound salmon fillet
> ½ cup extra virgin olive oil
> Salt and freshly ground black pepper, to taste
> 1 tablespoon champagne vinegar or white wine vinegar
> 1 tablespoon lemon juice
> 2 tablespoons chopped Italian flat-leaf parsley
> 2 tablespoons chopped fresh tarragon
> 1 large (1 pound) round country loaf, cut in half horizontally
> 2 cups trimmed arugula
> 1 jar (7 ounces) roasted red peppers, drained
> ½ cup thinly sliced red onion

Preheat the grill or broiler. Brush the salmon with 1 tablespoon of the olive oil and sprinkle with salt and pepper. Grill or broil until just cooked through, about 8 minutes per inch of thickness. Set aside.

Combine the vinegar, lemon juice, parsley, tarragon, the remaining 7 tablespoons oil, salt, and pepper in a jar with a tight-fitting lid. Shake until well combined.

Pull out most of the inside of the bread, leaving a wall about ½ inch thick. (Save the inside pieces for bread crumbs or croutons.) Brush the walls liberally with some of the dressing. Spread about half the arugula on the bottom of the bread, covering the entire bottom. Break the salmon into chunks and press *down over the arugula. Brush with more of the dressing. Top with the peppers, onions, and remaining arugula. Place the top over and wrap the entire bread tightly in foil. Refrigerate overnight.*

Before serving, let come to room temperature and cut the bread into wedges.

MACRINA BAKERY AND CAFE

Seattle, Washington

From a storefront shop in Seattle's Belltown, Leslie Mackie makes and sells handmade artisan breads, panini, and pastries. Her neighborhood bakery, Macrina, supplies local restaurants, a few specialty food markets, and its own cafe and retail bakery. Walk in any morning and you'll be surrounded by customers stopping in for their daily latte and breakfast. After several years as the head baker at Grand Central Bakery, Leslie set out on her own. She developed new bread recipes, each with its own special starter. These starters were the key to the complex tastes and textures she sought. The Casera loaf (a rustic loaf marked with a branch of olives) is a crusty brown bread leavened with a starter of backyard grapes. The Vollkorn, a German-style whole-grain bread, is leavened with starter made from a friend's homebrew. Each Macrina bread variety has a character and texture all its own. Macrina's fame spread beyond Seattle when Leslie appeared in the PBS television series *Baking with Julia*, and her recipes were included in the accompaning volume. Fame has not gone to her head, however. When asked, she describes herself as "originator, head baker, owner, and pot washer" of Macrina Bakery and Cafe.

Macrina's Ham and Cheese Panini

Serves 4

Macrina Bakery in Seattle is a neighborhood bakery offering artisan-style loaves, breakfast pastries, and panini, or Italian-style sandwiches. Macrina's owner, Leslie Mackie, bakes special panini loaves, but you can use 14-inch baguettes, split lengthwise.

½ large red onion, thinly sliced
1 tablespoon chopped Italian flat-leaf parsley
1 tablespoon balsamic vinegar
3 tablespoons extra virgin olive oil
Pinch of crushed red pepper
Coarse salt and freshly ground black pepper, to taste
3 plum tomatoes, thinly sliced
2 baguettes, split lengthwise
1 tablespoon Dijon mustard
12 slices Black Forest ham (about 8 ounces)
16 large basil leaves
6 slices Italian fontina (about 4 ounces)

Combine the onion, parsley, vinegar, 2 tablespoons of the olive oil, red pepper, and salt and pepper in a large bowl. Let stand at room temperature for 20 minutes.

In a small bowl, combine the tomatoes, the remaining olive oil, and salt and pepper. Set aside.

Spread the bottoms of the baguettes with the ham, the onion mixture, tomatoes, basil, and fontina. Spread the inside of the tops of the baguettes with the mustard and place on top of the cheese. Cut in half crosswise. If not serving immediately, wrap in wax paper to prevent drying out. Serve at room temperature.

Marinated Steak Sandwiches with Yellow Pepper Ketchup

Serves 4

Though steak is not as much a mainstay as it once was, a good steak sandwich is always welcome. It's particularly good on a flavorful artisan roll. Make the Yellow Pepper Ketchup a few days ahead and refrigerate it. Marinate the steak the night before. When you're ready to eat, simply fire up the grill.

3 cloves garlic, minced
6 scallions, minced
¼ cup olive oil
½ cup dry red wine
¼ cup soy sauce
1 teaspoon ground cumin
1½ pounds trimmed flank steak
½ teaspoon salt
½ teaspoon freshly ground black pepper
4 large white or sourdough rolls, split
2 cups shredded romaine
Yellow Pepper Ketchup (recipe follows)
¼ cup chopped cilantro

Combine the garlic, scallions, oil, wine, soy sauce, and cumin in a resealable plastic bag. Add the steak and seal. Marinate in the refrigerator for at least 4 hours or up to 24 hours.

Preheat the grill or broiler. Remove the steak and pat dry. Sprinkle with the salt and pepper and grill to desired doneness, about 4 to 5 minutes per side for medium rare. Let steak rest for 5 minutes.

Toast the rolls, cut sides down, until golden brown. Thinly slice the steak on an angle across the grain. Spread the bottoms of the rolls with the romaine, dividing evenly. Top with the steak slices and pepper ketchup and sprinkle with the cilantro. Top with the tops of the rolls and serve.

Yellow Pepper Ketchup

Makes 2 cups

2 yellow bell peppers, roasted, peeled, and seeded
1 medium onion, chopped
1 large clove garlic, minced
½ cup apple cider vinegar
2 tablespoons canola oil
2 tablespoons brown sugar
¼ teaspoon salt
¼ teaspoon minced canned chipotle chili in adobo sauce

Coarsely chop the peppers and combine with the remaining ingredients in a medium saucepan. Bring to a boil, reduce the heat, and simmer, covered, stirring occasionally, for 30 minutes or until the vegetables are tender. Transfer to a food processor and process until smooth. Chill at least 2 hours or up to 2 days.

ROASTING PEPPERS

Roast the pepper or peppers on the grill or broiler or over the open flame of a gas burner until blackened on all sides, about 15 minutes. In an electric stove, broil the pepper 2 to 3 inches from the heat source, turning to blacken all sides. Place the pepper in a paper bag and let cool. Using a paring knife, scrape off and discard the blackened skin. Stem and seed the pepper.

Northwest Grilled Cheese Sandwich

Serves 1

Every cuisine has some kind of grilled cheese, be it quesadillas, Croque Monsieur, or Cuban sandwiches. This grilled cheese, based on crusty Grand Central yeasted cornbread and Washington State University's fabulous Cougar Gold cheese, is Gwen Bassetti's inspiration. A list of suggestions for other grilled cheese sandwiches, both plain and fanciful, follows.

> *1 tablespoon unsalted butter, softened*
> *2 slices (½-inch thick) yeasted cornbread*
> *4 thin slices Cougar Gold cheese*
> *1 to 2 tablespoons salsa, well drained*
> *1 tablespoon chopped cilantro*

Spread the butter on 1 slice of the bread and place it, butter side down, on a cutting board. Place the cheese on top of the slice, top it with salsa and cilantro and place the remaining slice of bread on top. Heat a heavy skillet, preferably cast-iron, over medium-high heat and place the sandwich in the skillet, butter side down. Weight down with another skillet, a plate loaded down with a can, or a teakettle filled with water. Cook until golden brown on the bottom, 1 to 2 minutes. Flip over and weight down again. Cook 1 to 2 minutes more, or until golden brown on the other side. Cut in half on the diagonal and serve.

VARIATIONS ON THE GRILLED CHEESE SANDWICH
(USE ANY BREAD YOU FANCY FOR THESE COMBINATIONS):

> *Asiago or Italian fontina, prosciutto, and thinly sliced tomato*
> *Brie and Mushroom Tapenade (see page 31)*
> *Brie, Dijon mustard, smoked turkey, and thinly sliced cucumber*
> *Camembert, cucumber, and shredded radicchio*
> *Cheddar and arugula*
> *Cheddar, sautéed mushrooms, and apples*
> *Italian fontina and sautéed fennel*

Italian fontina, tomato, and arugula
Gorgonzola and sautéed pears
Gorgonzola and lightly sautéed zucchini slices
Gruyère, smoked Gouda, Parmesan, and baby spinach leaves
Gruyère, ham, honey mustard, tomato, and chopped tarragon
Jalapeño cheese, refried beans, sliced avocado, and cilantro
Jarlsberg, ham, roasted pork, yellow mustard, and red onion
Monterey jack, bacon, avocado, and tomato
Mozzarella or asiago, coppa, and chopped parsley and basil
Smoked mozzarella, Walla Walla onion, tomato, and basil
Provolone and marinated roasted peppers

FLOUR POWER

Wheat grown in North America is commonly classified as spring or winter wheat, referring to the time of year it is planted. Winter wheat is actually planted in the fall and winters over. Spring plantings are common in more severe winter areas. The terms hard and soft indicate the relative protein content in the grain. Higher-protein hard wheat has more gluten-forming compounds, which trap the gases created by fermentation; it is ideal for bread. Soft wheat, which is lower in protein, is the choice for cakes and cookies.

The relatively mild winters of the wheat-growing regions of the Northwest favor winter wheat, which is generally soft. The Asian markets served from the ports of Seattle and Portland provide a ready market for soft wheat, which is used there to make noodles. Most hard, spring wheat is grown in the northern plains of the United States and Canada.

THE VILLAGE BAKERY

Port Hadlock, Washington

André LeRest and his wife, Beth, were both home bakers. The only way French-born André could get the bread his blood demanded while living in Port Townsend, Washington, was to bake it himself. He and Beth gave bread to friends, and those friends, perhaps hoping to keep the supply coming and their consciences clear, eventually insisted on paying. In October of 1994, André officially opened a bakery in nearby Port Hadlock, figuring that if Beth kept her job they could make ends meet. In two years time Beth had taken a leave and they were planning for expansion. They soon moved into an attractive market complex located a mile from the original bakery. A new hearth oven has made the LeRest's baking life a bit more complex. Prior to the move they mixed and formed on odd-numbered days, baked and delivered on even-numbered days, taking Sundays off and closing in January. All with one employee. Now they have five employees, a truck, and bake six days a week.

French regional specialties at the Village Bakery include pain plié, a traditional bread of Brittany which is folded like an oversize Parker House roll, and pain de Lodève or paillasse, named for the basket in which the dough is proofed. True to the tradition of French regional breads, André's loaves are made from a basic light dough, taking their unique character and flavor from the shape. André makes a baguette of course, but it is slightly heavier than the French government standard. He uses the *poolish* method for a loaf that lasts longer than the average Parisian baguette.

Pan-Asian Tuna Sandwich

Serves 4

The Northwest is famous for its fusion cuisine. Here's an Asian-inspired tuna salad sandwich. Look for wasabi powder at large supermarkets and specialty stores.

4 large white or sourdough rolls, split lengthwise
½ pound tuna steak, cut ½ inch thick
1 tablespoon canola oil
Salt and freshly ground black pepper, to taste
1 tablespoon wasabi powder
½ medium cucumber, peeled, cut in half lengthwise,
*   seeded, and thinly sliced*
½ cup thinly sliced celery
¼ cup low-fat mayonnaise
1 teaspoon lime juice
2 cups watercress, trimmed

Preheat the grill or broiler. Toast the rolls, cut side up, until golden, 5 minutes. Set aside.

Brush the tuna with the oil and sprinkle with salt and pepper. Grill or broil until light pink on the inside, about 7 to 8 minutes per inch of thickness. Let rest for 5 minutes. Thinly slice on the diagonal.

In a medium bowl, stir together the wasabi powder and 1 tablespoon of water until it becomes a smooth paste. Add the cucumber, celery, mayonnaise, and lime juice. Season with salt and pepper.

Spread the bottoms of the rolls with the watercress, dividing evenly. Top with the tuna slices, wasabi mixture, and the tops of the rolls. Serve immediately.

Main Courses

Panfried Crumbed Oysters with Roasted Tomatillo Salsa

Serves 4

As the top oyster-producing region in the United States, the Northwest grows oysters of every shape and size. Any type of small oyster will work well in this recipe, as long as they are exceedingly fresh. Make some coleslaw and oven-roasted sweet potato fries to complete the meal, as well as this easy green salsa.

> *¼ cup all-purpose flour*
> *1 large egg*
> *Salt and freshly ground black pepper*
> *1 cup fine dry bread crumbs, made from sourdough or*
> *   white bread*
> *¼ cup cornmeal*
> *Vegetable oil for frying*
> *2 jars (10 ounces each) freshly shucked small oysters*
> *Roasted Tomatillo Salsa (recipe follows)*

Put the flour in a pie plate and the egg in another one. Beat the egg with 1 tablespoon water and a large pinch of salt and pepper until well mixed. Put the bread crumbs in a third pie plate and stir in the cornmeal.

Heat ½ inch of oil in a large skillet over medium-high heat, or until a cube of bread cooks in about 40 seconds. Dip each oyster in flour, then in the egg. Let the excess drip off, then dredge in the bread crumb mixture. Slip into the oil. Repeat with the remaining oysters, frying 4 or 5 at a time until golden brown on both sides, turning once. Transfer to paper towels with a slotted spoon. Keep warm in a low oven until all the oysters are done. Sprinkle the oysters with more salt if desired and serve at once with the salsa.

Roasted Tomatillo Salsa

Makes 1 cup

> *8 medium tomatillos (about 8 ounces)*
> *½ to 1 medium jalapeño, seeded and chopped*
> *½ cup chopped Walla Walla onion*
> *2 cloves garlic, minced*
> *2 tablespoons fresh lime juice*
> *3 tablespoons chopped cilantro*
> *Pinch of salt*

Preheat the broiler.

Place the tomatillos on a baking sheet and broil 2 to 3 inches from the heat source, until the tomatillos are blackened on one side, about 5 to 7 minutes. Turn over and blacken on the other side. Let cool. Transfer to a food processor and add the jalapeño, onion, and garlic. Process to a chunky puree. Stir in the lime juice, cilantro, and salt.

Mussel and Potato Gratin

Serves 4

Three types of mussels are common to Northwest waters: blue or black mussels (also known as Penn Coves), wild Pacific mussels, and the larger Mediterranean mussels. Since Mediterranean mussels are at their peak in summer, when the others are not, there is always a good supply here. In this recipe, the mussels are cooked lightly, then baked with layers of potatoes, onion, garlic, and a bit of saffron-flavored heavy cream.

24 Penn Cove, Mediterranean, or Pacific mussels
1½ pounds Yukon Gold potatoes
1 large Walla Walla or yellow onion, thinly sliced
3 cloves garlic, minced
2 large ripe tomatoes, seeded and chopped
¼ cup chopped fresh basil
Salt and freshly ground black pepper
¼ cup extra virgin olive oil
¼ cup heavy cream
1 large pinch ground saffron or ⅛ teaspoon saffron threads
2 cups coarse fresh bread crumbs, made from sourdough,
*   rosemary, or olive bread*
½ cup grated Pecorino Romano

Put the mussels in a medium saucepan over high heat. Cover and cook until the mussels start to open, 3 to 4 minutes. Remove them with a slotted spoon or tongs as they open. Reserve the mussel liquid. Let the mussels cool slightly and remove from the shells. Discard the shells, cover the mussels, and set aside.

Meanwhile, put the potatoes in a medium saucepan, cover with cold water, and bring to a boil. Reduce the heat and simmer, covered, until tender, 15 to 20 minutes. Drain and let cool slightly. Peel and thinly slice.

Preheat the oven to 450°F. Lightly oil a 13 x 9-inch baking dish.

Layer half the potatoes over the bottom of the dish, then half of the onion, all the garlic, and all the mussels. Top with half of the tomatoes, 2 tablespoons of basil, and a generous sprinkling of salt and pepper. Drizzle with 1 tablespoon of the olive oil and top with the remaining potatoes, onion, tomatoes, and basil. Sprinkle generously with salt and pepper. Mix together the cream, the reserved mussel liquid, and the saffron. Pour over the gratin. Combine the bread crumbs, Pecorino Romano, and the remaining 3 tablespoons olive oil in a small bowl and sprinkle over the top.

Bake in the upper half of the oven for 25 minutes, or until the bread crumbs are nicely browned. Let sit for 5 minutes before serving.

Spot Prawns with Fennel Bread Stuffing

Serves 4

Spot prawns are large, wonderful, sweet-tasting prawns from Alaska, Oregon, and Washington State waters. In this dish, they are stuffed and quickly roasted on top of a fennel, zucchini, and tomato base.

1 teaspoon fennel seeds

1 clove garlic

¼ teaspoon each salt and freshly ground pepper

4½ tablespoons extra virgin olive oil

1⅓ cups fine fresh bread crumbs, made from Italian white bread

1 teaspoon grated orange zest

2 tablespoons chopped Italian flat-leaf parsley

1½ teaspoons chopped fresh basil

1 pound (about 12) spot prawns or extra-large shrimp, unpeeled

1 large egg, lightly beaten

1 large fennel, fronds reserved, quartered and very thinly sliced

1 pound medium zucchini, cut into 2-inch pieces, then thinly sliced into 2- to 3-inch lengths

2 tablespoons Chicken Broth (page 57) or vegetable broth

2 plum tomatoes, seeded and finely chopped

Toast the fennel seeds in a medium skillet over medium-high heat until fragrant, about 2 minutes. Transfer to a cutting board and chop together with the garlic and salt until very finely minced. Heat 1½ tablespoons of the oil in the same skillet and add the fennel mixture. Sauté until fragrant, about 30 seconds. Stir in the bread crumbs, orange zest, parsley, basil, and pepper. Transfer to a bowl and set aside to cool.

Preheat the oven to 400°F.

Using kitchen scissors, split each prawn shell down the back. Then using the scissors or a paring knife and cutting from front to back, make a deep lengthwise slit, cutting about three quarters of the way through the prawn. Rinse and devein if desired. Dry the prawns well and refrigerate.

Stir the egg into the stuffing mixture and place a heaping teaspoonful into the slit of each prawn. Using your fingers, press the stuffing into the prawn to secure it. Repeat with the remaining stuffing and prawns and refrigerate.

Place the fennel, zucchini, 2 tablespoons of the remaining olive oil, ½ teaspoon salt, ½ teaspoon pepper, and the broth in a 13 x 9-inch baking dish. Toss to mix, cover, and bake for 30 minutes. Uncover and bake for 20 minutes more, or until the vegetables are very tender. Remove from the oven. Turn on the broiler.

Place the prawns on top of the vegetables (they won't stand up). Chop 2 tablespoons of the reserved fennel fronds and toss with the tomatoes and the remaining 1 tablespoon oil. Sprinkle over the prawns. Broil until the prawns are cooked and the stuffing is slightly browned, about 3 to 5 minutes longer. Serve immediately.

Parmesan-Breaded Sea Bass with Parsley Mayonnaise

Serves 4

Chilean sea bass is an amazing mild fish with an unctuous texture. Here it's breaded with very fine fresh bread crumbs (no crusts please) mixed with a bit of Parmigiano-Reggiano, and panfried until crisp on the outside and soft and buttery on the inside. Pair it with this easy Parsley Mayonnaise.

1 large egg
Salt and freshly ground black pepper
⅓ cup all-purpose flour
⅔ cup very fine fresh bread crumbs, made from Italian white bread
⅓ cup finely grated Parmigiano-Reggiano
4 fillets (4 to 6 ounces each) sea bass, true cod, monkfish,
    or black cod
3 tablespoons extra virgin olive oil
Parsley Mayonnaise (recipe follows)

Put the flour in a pie plate and the egg in another one. Whisk the egg with 1 tablespoon water and a large pinch of salt and pepper. Combine the bread crumbs and Parmigiano-Reggiano in a third pie plate and mix well. Dip both sides of the fillets in the flour and shake off any excess. Dip the fillets in the egg and let the excess drip off. Coat in the bread crumb mixture and place on a rack. Repeat with the remaining fillets.

Heat the oil over medium-high heat until hot, but not smoking. Sauté the fillets until golden brown, 3 to 4 minutes per side, turning once. Serve immediately with the Parsley Mayonnaise on the side.

Variation: Substitute lightly pounded boneless and skinless chicken breasts for the fish.

Parsley Mayonnaise

Makes ¾ cup

¾ cup prepared mayonnaise
2 tablespoons minced Italian flat-leaf parsley
1 large shallot, minced
1 teaspoon grated lemon zest

Combine the mayonnaise, parsley, shallot, and lemon zest in a small bowl and mix well. Set aside for 1 hour to let the flavors meld.

PARMESAN

Buying real Parmigiano-Reggiano by the wedge is the best way to go. Wrap it well, and it will retain its flavor for months. You can grate it, shred it on the large holes of a grater, or make large, thin flakes with a vegetable peeler. Shave the flakes onto a plate or piece of wax paper and toss them on the top of mushrooms, pasta, or bruschetta.

Pasta Shells with Salmon, Tomatoes, and Toasted Bread Crumbs

Serves 4

This summery pasta dish with tomatoes, salmon, and herbs is topped with whole wheat bread crumbs. It's quite a common practice in Italy to add bread crumbs to pasta, especially when the crumbs stand in for cheese. Whole wheat crumbs make a nice contrast to the acidity of the tomatoes and the oiliness of the fish, but feel free to substitute white country or sourdough bread crumbs instead.

½ cup extra virgin olive oil

8 plum tomatoes, seeded and cut into ¾-inch cubes

1 large clove garlic, minced

¼ cup chopped mint

2 tablespoons lemon juice

1½ teaspoons grated lemon zest

Pinch of crushed red pepper

Salt and freshly ground black pepper

1½ cups coarse fresh whole wheat bread crumbs

¾ pound salmon fillet, pin bones removed

1 pound large pasta shells

Combine 5 tablespoons of the olive oil, the tomatoes, garlic, mint, lemon juice, lemon zest, red pepper, 1 teaspoon salt, and ½ teaspoon pepper in a large pasta bowl. Stir to mix and set aside.

Preheat the grill or broiler. Bring a large pot of water to a boil.

Heat 2 tablespoons of the olive oil in a medium skillet over medium-high heat. Add the bread crumbs and stir until toasted and crisp, about 5 minutes. Season with salt and pepper and set aside.

Brush the salmon with the remaining 1 tablespoon oil and season with salt and pepper. Grill or broil the salmon, about 4 minutes. Turn and cook 3 to 5 minutes more, or until cooked through. Remove to a plate and break into chunks.

Cook the pasta shells until al dente and drain. Transfer to the bowl with the tomatoes and add the salmon. Toss to mix and sprinkle with the bread crumbs. Serve immediately.

ECCO IL PANE

Vancouver, British Columbia

A massive wood-fired oven sets an Old World tone at this upscale neighborhood bakery/bistro on West Broadway. Owners are the husband-and-wife team of Pamela Gaudreault and Christopher Brown. As a chef, Christopher had always enjoyed making simple artisan breads for himself but was disappointed in what was commercially available. Then, while working in Italy, he volunteered several nights a week in a tiny bakery in Florence. As he was sitting in the kitchen in the early morning hours with a glass of red wine and a slice of fall harvest bread, inspiration came. "The only way to do better than this," he thought, "is to do it ourselves!" After retiring from the Royal Winnepeg Ballet, Pamela had owned a small cake shop called Au Beau Gâteau, so a jump to *biscotti* and *dolci* was easy. A favorite bread at Ecco il Pane is their Casa, a long rustic loaf made with whole wheat and durum flour, a loaf that has definite roots in Florence.

Roast Chicken with Winter Squash, Currants, and Sourdough Bread Stuffing

Serves 5 to 6

Butternut squash and dried currants make an unexpected and sweet addition to the usual bread stuffing. Make this chicken at the end of summer when squash is starting to come in and you still have plenty of sage in your garden.

4 slices bacon, chopped
1 cup chopped red onion
1½ teaspoons chopped fresh thyme leaves or ½ teaspoon
    dried thyme
1 tablespoon chopped fresh sage leaves or 1 teaspoon dried sage
1 small (about ¾ pound) butternut squash, peeled, seeded, and
    cut into ¾-inch cubes (about 1½ cups)
1½ cups Chicken Broth (page 57)
5 thick (1-inch) slices stale sourdough or Italian white bread,
    cut into 1-inch cubes (5 to 6 cups)
¼ cup dried currants
Salt and freshly ground black pepper, to taste
1 large roasting chicken (about 5 pounds)
¼ cup extra virgin olive oil
8 small onions, peeled
8 carrots, peeled, halved lengthwise, and cut into 2-inch lengths
16 small red potatoes, scrubbed and cut in half (about 1 pound)
8 sage sprigs (optional)

Cook the bacon in a large skillet over medium-high heat until crisp, stirring frequently, about 10 minutes. Remove to paper towels with a slotted spoon. Stir in the chopped onion and cook, stirring frequently, 4 to 5 minutes. Stir in the thyme, chopped sage, squash, and broth and bring to a boil. Reduce the heat to a simmer and cook, covered, for 8 minutes, or until the squash is very tender. Stir in the bread, bacon, and currants and season with salt and pepper to taste. Set aside to cool.

Preheat the oven to 450°F.

Loosely fill the chicken cavity with the stuffing and truss the chicken. Place the remaining stuffing in a baking dish and cover with foil. Brush the chicken with 1 tablespoon of the olive oil and season with salt and pepper. Place, breast side up, on a rack set in a large roasting pan. Toss the onions, carrots, potatoes, and sage sprigs in a large bowl with the remaining oil and season with salt and pepper. Scatter the vegetables around the chicken.

Roast for 1½ hours, or until the juices from the thigh run clear when pricked with a knife. About 30 minutes before the chicken is done, place the baking dish with the remaining stuffing in the oven. When the chicken is ready, remove from the oven, cover with foil, and let rest for 10 minutes. Transfer to a cutting board and carve. Serve the chicken with the stuffing, vegetables, and sage sprigs.

Grilled Game Hens with Olive Bread Stuffing

Serves 4

Olive bread transforms itself into a fabulous stuffing. Locally made loaves are filled with lots of juicy kalamata olives and scented with herbs. Of course, you can buy any artisan bread you like for this stuffing and simply add olives, but why make extra work? Serve these hens with Baked Stuffed Tomatoes (page 95).

> ¼ cup extra virgin olive oil
> 1 medium onion, chopped
> 2 cloves garlic, minced
> 2 tablespoons chopped fresh basil
> 1½ teaspoons grated lemon zest
> 2 tablespoons toasted pine nuts, chopped
> 3½ cups ¾-inch cubes olive bread (about 5 ounces)
> ½ cup homemade Chicken Broth (page 57), or
>   low-sodium canned broth
> 2 tablespoons grated Parmesan
> Salt and freshly ground black pepper, to taste
> 2 Cornish game hens (about 1½ pounds each)

Heat 3 tablespoons of the oil in a large skillet over medium-high heat. Add the onion and cook, stirring frequently, until soft, 3 to 4 minutes. Stir in the garlic, basil, lemon zest, pine nuts, and olive bread and cook until the garlic is fragrant, about 1 minute. Stir in the broth and simmer until it is absorbed by the bread, about 5 minutes. Stir in the Parmesan and season with salt and pepper to taste. Set aside and let cool.

Preheat the grill or broiler.

Open each of the game hens by cutting up the back parallel to the backbone. Remove the backbone and with the heel of your hand, pressing down firmly on the breast to flatten the hens. Beginning at the neck end, very gently slide your fingers under the skin to separate the skin from the meat.

Spread the stuffing mixture evenly over the meat under the skin. Brush the hens with the remaining 1 tablespoon oil and season the skin with salt and pepper.

Grill the hens, skin side up, for 12 to 15 minutes over medium-low heat. Turn and grill 10 to 12 minutes longer, or until the juices from the thigh run clear when pricked with a knife. Let stand, covered, for 5 minutes. With poultry shears or a large knife, halve each bird and serve.

TERRA BREADS

Vancouver, British Columbia

Michael Lansky and his co-owner and head baker, Mary Mackay, opened Terra in 1993, creating an immediate destination for bread-hungry Vancouverites. Working primarily with natural starters, Terra offers a large selection of breads and an array of appealing rustic pastries. The retail storefront affords a full view of the hearth oven in operation.

Specialties include a classic pain au levain, the naturally leavened dark bread of the French countryside. The focaccia selection changes from day to day. Fougasse, or ladder bread, comes in several garlic-studded sizes, and an original bread with figs and anise is a specialty. Terra Breads also has a location in the Granville Island public market, where shoppers and tourists alike crowd shoulder to shoulder on busy Saturday mornings to watch the spectacle of the baker at work.

Rack of Lamb with Pomegranate Marinade and Walnut Crumbs

Serves 4

Although rack of lamb is a common item on restaurant menus, it's not usually prepared at home. The rack (the rib section of the lamb) is a wonderful cut of meat, easily purchased from a butcher, who will also crack it between the bones for easy carving, trim it, and "French" it if you request. ("Frenching" consists of trimming off all the fat and meat from between the ribs, leaving a very elegant presentation.) Here, it's marinated in a powerful blend of garlic, pomegranate molasses, red wine, and ground coriander. After roasting, the meat is crisp and brown on the outside, tender, moist, and rare on the inside.

3 large cloves garlic, minced

¼ cup chopped cilantro

3 tablespoons dry red wine

1 teaspoon ground coriander

1 tablespoon pomegranate molasses (see Note)

½ cup plus 2 tablespoons extra virgin olive oil

2 racks of lamb, 7 or 8 ribs each, trimmed

3 tablespoons finely chopped walnuts

1 cup fine fresh bread crumbs, made from crustless
   Italian white or sourdough bread

¾ teaspoon salt

¾ teaspoon freshly ground black pepper

Combine the garlic, cilantro, wine, coriander, pomegranate molasses, and ½ cup olive oil in a shallow pan. Add the racks of lamb and turn to coat. Cover and marinate, refrigerated, overnight.

Remove the lamb from the refrigerator. Preheat the oven to 450°F and adjust the oven rack to the middle level.

Mix the walnuts, bread crumbs, the remaining 2 tablespoons olive oil, and ¼ teaspoon each salt and pepper in a small bowl. Heat a large ovenproof skillet over high heat. Remove the lamb from the marinade and pat dry. Brown it quickly on all sides, about 1 minute per side. Pat the bread crumb mixture firmly over the top fat. Roast for 15 minutes for medium rare. Remove from the oven and let rest for 5 minutes before carving.

Note: Pomegranate molasses is available at Pacific Food Importers or The Souk (both in Seattle) or by mail order from Dean and DeLuca, 560 Broadway, New York, NY 10012, (800) 221-7714 or (212) 431-1691; Kalustyan, 123 Lexington Ave., New York, NY 10016, (212) 685-3416; and Persian markets. Keep the opened bottle in a cool, dark place.

Spaghetti with Caramelized Walla Walla
Onions, Olives, and Rosemary Bread Crumbs

Serves 4

Make this pasta in the summer when Walla Wallas are at their peak. Slow cooking turns them tender and incredibly sweet. Salty olives, sharp Pecorino Romano, and bread crumbs perfumed with rosemary balance all those honeyed onions. Make sure you use the largest skillet you own (12-inch is best) for sautéing the onions.

> *5 tablespoons extra virgin olive oil*
> *6 large Walla Walla onions, peeled, cut in half lengthwise and*
>   *thinly sliced, (about 4½ pounds)*
> *1 teaspoon sugar*
> *3 cloves garlic, minced*
> *Salt and freshly ground black pepper, to taste*
> *12 large kalamata olives, pitted and chopped*
> *2 cups large, chunky fresh bread crumbs, made from sourdough*
>   *or light whole wheat bread*
> *1 tablespoon chopped fresh rosemary*
> *½ cup grated Pecorino Romano*
> *1 pound spaghetti*

Heat 3 tablespoons of the olive oil in a large skillet over medium-high heat. Add the onions and a pinch of sugar and cook, stirring occasionally, until the onions are very tender and sweet, about 20 minutes. Stir in the garlic, salt, pepper, and olives. Keep warm.

Heat the remaining 2 tablespoons oil in a small skillet over medium-high heat. Add the bread crumbs and rosemary and stir until browned and crisp, about 7 minutes. Stir in the Pecorino Romano and season with salt and pepper. Set aside.

Bring a large pot of water to a boil. Add salt to taste and the spaghetti and cook until al dente. Transfer to a serving dish and scrape the onions on top. Sprinkle with the bread crumbs. Serve at once.

ANJOU BAKERY

Cashmere, Washington

In eastern Washington, pioneer orchard towns follow one another down the Wenatchee River. Amid the dry hills and lush green orchards is the hamlet of Cashmere. And just beyond the turn for Cashmere itself, a sign posted high in a pear tree announces, "Anjou Bakery, turn here."

Proprietors Heather and Kevin Knight are émigrés from Bainbridge Island. Together they produce Anjou Bakery's 70 to 100 loaves a day, plus a variety of appealing pastries. All this is accomplished with a 30-quart mixer and a single Blodgett convection oven lined with tiles and cleverly "plumbed for steam" using a system powered by a small hand pressure sprayer.

The building, nestled among the pear trees, is a remodeled fruit warehouse that doubles as both bakery and family home for Heather and Kevin and their two boys. They operate every day but Sunday, which takes a lot of running up and down stairs as retail customers announce themselves over the baby monitor that serves as the intercom from the retail area to the tidy basement bakery.

Anjou uses all natural starters, and the Knights try to use organic flour when possible, along with the best-quality ingredients in their ten varieties of bread. A three-dollar loaf of bread is still a novelty in this small town, but Kevin's Normandy wheat, country white, and walnut rye loaves are regularly making converts.

Baked Stuffed Tomatoes

Serves 4

Traditionally, these stuffed tomatoes are flavored with Provençal herbs. Here they've taken a Tex-Mex turn with the additions of cilantro and jalapeño. Serve as garnish or vegetable side dish.

4 firm ripe tomatoes, cut crosswise in half
Salt
½ cup fine fresh bread crumbs, made from sourdough,
*   white, light whole wheat, or Italian bread*
1 clove garlic, minced
½ to 1 medium jalapeño, seeded and minced
2 tablespoons chopped cilantro
1 tablespoon finely chopped red onion
½ teaspoon freshly ground black pepper
2 tablespoons canola oil

Preheat the oven to 400°F.

Poke the seeds out of the tomatoes with your fingers and sprinkle the cut sides lightly with salt. Turn over and let drain for 10 minutes on paper towels.

Combine the bread crumbs, garlic, jalapeño, cilantro, onion, pepper, a pinch of salt, and the oil in a small bowl. Mix well and pat onto the cut sides of the tomatoes. Place on a baking sheet and bake until browned and bubbling, 20 to 25 minutes. Serve hot or at room temperature.

BAKERS' WORDS

Banneton: The basket, often cloth lined, in which some breads are proofed after forming.

Biga: Italian for starter.

Couche: The canvas that cradles a baguette or bâtard after shaping and through the final proof.

Dividing and scaling: Cutting and weighing dough prior to molding.

Flour: Any powdery foodstuff that is the result of grinding and sifting, especially wheat used for baking. Flour is available in endless varieties and blends tailored to specific baking requirements.

Gluten: A plant protein contained in wheat that, when mixed with water, forms an elastic, "gluey" network that traps the gases created by fermentation.

Kissers: Two loaves, which when placed too close on the hearth, join together while baking.

Levain: French for starter. A *levain* is a piece of dough set aside to use as leavening for the next batch of bread.

Molding: Shaping or forming of the dough into a loaf.

Oven spring: The last burst of energy from the leavening when the loaf hits the oven heat.

Peel: A long-handled shovel-like tool used to move loaves in and out of a hearth oven.

Poolish: French term for something between a sponge and a biga. Adapted from a process introduced in Poland in the nineteenth century, hence the name.

Pre-ferment: Any one of various doughs, such as starter, sponge, or *poolish,* used as leavening for a final dough. Terms and techniques vary and interpretations often overlap.

Proof: A single stage of fermentation of a dough or formed loaf prior to baking. Sometimes a proof box, a controlled-temperature chamber, is used to regulate proofing time.

Retard: The process of slowing fermentation in order to develop flavor and texture by refrigerating the dough.

Score: The cut made in a loaf prior to baking. It relieves the surface tension and allows for the final burst of leavening when the loaf goes in the oven. The pattern of the score affects the final shape of the loaf and becomes part of that loaf's identification.

Sponge: A pre-ferment that includes the yeast, the liquid, and up to half of the flour in the formula.

Starter: The term used most commonly to indicate a pre-ferment that has been developed slowly by enticing wild yeast spores to take residence in dough. Such natural starters sometimes develop flavors unique to their environment.

Stone: A ceramic or porous stone insert for the home oven that simulates the hearth of a baker's oven. Often sold as pizza stones.

Unbleached flour: The staple wheat flour for baking. Choose stone-ground white flour (with the germ, if possible) for basic bread.

Whole wheat flour: Whole wheat flour is ground from 100 percent of the wheat berry. Coarse-ground whole wheat flour is sometimes called graham flour after the man who first celebrated its health benefits.

Yeast: Single-celled fungi that cause fermentation of carbohydrates into carbon dioxide and alcohol. Dormant baker's yeast is available in moist cakes, dry, or active dry powder. All are recommended. Avoid fast-rising yeast, which is treated.

Breakfast and Brunch

Bread-Crumbed French Toast with Blackberry Maple Syrup

Serves 4

Officially known as pain perdu *(or lost bread), here's the perfect use for leftover loaves. An unusual rendition, this French toast recipe results in bread with a crisp, crunchy outside and a creamy, eggy interior. Try it with Grand Central's yeasted cornbread, a nut bread (walnut or hazelnut), challah, or even a whole wheat sourdough.*

3 large eggs
½ cup milk
Pinch of salt
⅔ cup fine dry bread crumbs
¼ cup cornmeal
4 tablespoons (½ stick) unsalted butter
8 slices (½-inch thick) artisan bread, such as yeasted cornbread,
  sourdough, or walnut bread
Blackberry Maple Syrup (recipe follows)

Preheat oven to 250°F.

Whisk together the eggs, milk, and salt in a pie plate. Combine the bread crumbs and cornmeal in another pie plate, until well mixed.

Melt 1 tablespoon of the butter in a large heavy skillet over medium heat. Dip the bread in the egg on both sides and let the excess drip off, then dredge in the bread crumb mixture. Fry as many slices at a time as will fit comfortably, until golden brown and crisp, 1 to 2 minutes per side, turning once. Keep warm in the oven until all the slices are cooked. Serve hot with the syrup.

Blackberry Maple Syrup

Makes 2 cups

1 teaspoon grated orange zest
2 cups fresh or frozen blackberries, blueberries, or raspberries
1 cup maple syrup

Combine the orange zest, berries, and maple syrup in a small saucepan. Bring to a simmer. Remove from heat, cover, and keep warm.

<u>Cinnamon and Cardamom Toast</u>

Serves 4

When was the last time you had cinnamon toast? Here's a grown-up version, spiked with cardamom, an aromatic spice beloved by many of the Northwest's Scandinavian descendants.

2 tablespoons sugar
¼ teaspoon ground cinnamon
¼ teaspoon ground cardamom
4 slices (½-inch thick) sourdough, whole wheat, walnut,
    or potato bread, or yeasted cornbread
2 tablespoons unsalted butter

Combine the sugar, cinnamon, and cardamom in a small bowl. Toast the bread on both sides and spread on one side with the butter. Sprinkle liberally with the sugar mixture and serve.

Scalloped Tomatoes

Serves 4

This side dish is easily made from pantry staples. Serve it for brunch with a strata or at dinner with a roast (it's particularly well suited to lamb). Bake the tomatoes in an attractive casserole and serve hot or warm.

¼ cup extra virgin olive oil

2 cups trimmed and cubed (½ inch) country white or sourdough bread, or rustic-style baguette

2 large cloves garlic, minced

12 ripe plum tomatoes, cut lengthwise into quarters and then into halves, or 1 can (28 ounces) drained plum tomatoes, cut similarly

1 tablespoon sugar

Salt and freshly ground black pepper, to taste

½ cup shredded fresh basil or 1 teaspoon dried basil

¼ cup grated Parmesan or other hard cheese

Preheat the oven to 350°F.

Heat 2 tablespoons of the oil in a large skillet over medium-high heat. Add the bread and toss to coat. Sauté until golden. Add the garlic, tomatoes, and sugar. Cook, stirring frequently, for 5 to 10 minutes, or until the tomatoes release their juices. Remove from the heat, stir in the basil, and season with salt and pepper. Transfer to a 1½-quart casserole. (The dish can be assembled up to several hours ahead to this point.) Sprinkle the grated cheese over the top and drizzle with the remaining olive oil.

Bake for 35 to 40 minutes, or until bubbly and browned. Serve hot or warm.

Grand Central Strata

Serves 6

This strata recipe from Gwen Bassetti results in a rich, savory bread pudding. Make it the night before company is coming and simply slip it into the oven as they arrive.

6 tablespoons (¾ stick) unsalted butter
½ cup chopped onion
4 ounces button or cremini mushrooms, thinly sliced
2 bunches (about 2 pounds) fresh spinach, stemmed, blanched, and
*   coarsely chopped, or 1 package (10 ounces) frozen chopped*
*   spinach, thawed*
2 tablespoons chopped fresh basil or 1 teaspoon dried basil
Salt and freshly ground black pepper, to taste
5 large eggs
4 cups half-and-half, milk, or a combination
1 loaf sourdough or Como bread, crusts removed and thinly sliced
1 cup shredded mozzarella
½ cup grated Parmesan

Melt 1 tablespoon of the butter in a large skillet over medium-high heat. Add the onions and mushrooms and sauté until soft, 4 to 5 minutes. Stir in the spinach and basil and season with salt and pepper. Set aside to cool.

Whisk the eggs in a large bowl until well mixed. Whisk in the half-and-half and season with salt and pepper.

Grease a 8½ x 11-inch or 9 x 13-inch baking dish and cut the bread to cover the bottom, with the pieces fitting snugly. Spread the vegetable mixture over the bread and top with the mozzarella and Parmesan. Pour the egg mixture over and top with the remaining bread. (For a decorative effect, cut the bread into triangles and arrange in a pattern.) Press lightly into the egg mixture and dot with the remaining butter. Cover and refrigerate overnight or for at least 2 hours.

Preheat the oven to 350°F.

Place the baking dish in a larger roasting pan and fill the pan with hot water halfway up the baking dish.

Bake until browned on top, about 50 to 60 minutes. Let stand for 5 minutes before cutting.

Asparagus with Poached Eggs, Garlic Croûtes, and Baby Greens

Serves 4

Brunch poses a tricky question: Does it call for breakfast or lunch food? This recipe answers perfectly. The combination of soft poached eggs dripping over steamed asparagus and crunchy, garlicky bread is irresistible.

1 pound thin asparagus, washed and trimmed

Salt to taste

4 to 8 large eggs

4 large slices (½-inch thick) sourdough or light whole wheat bread, or yeasted cornbread

2 cloves garlic, cut in half

3 tablespoons extra virgin olive oil

12 plum tomatoes, chopped

1 tablespoon minced shallot

1 teaspoon chopped fresh thyme leaves

5 cups mixed baby greens

2 teaspoons champagne vinegar

Freshly ground black pepper, to taste

¼ cup large shavings of Parmigiano-Reggiano

Preheat the grill or broiler.

Bring 1 inch of water to a boil in a large skillet and add the asparagus and salt to taste. Simmer, covered, until the asparagus is cooked, 5 to 6 minutes. Using a slotted spoon, transfer to a plate and keep warm.

Bring 3 to 4 inches of water to a simmer in a medium saucepan. Poach the eggs for 2 minutes or to desired doneness. Using a slotted spoon, transfer to paper towels.

Toast the bread until brown on both sides and rub with the cut sides of the garlic. Brush with 1 tablespoon of the olive oil and place on 4 serving plates. Top with the asparagus and place 1 or 2 eggs on top of the asparagus.

Mix together the tomatoes, shallot, thyme, greens, vinegar, and the remaining 2 tablespoons olive oil in a large mixing bowl. Sprinkle with salt and pepper and mix well. Place handfuls of the salad on either side of the plate and divide the cheese among of the portions. Serve immediately.

BREAD OVENS

Archaeological clues tell us that the development of ovens and risen breads occurred together. The first breads were presumably simple pastes of flour and water, cooked on a flat surface. Once leavening was introduced, the early baker quickly discovered that the results could be improved by covering the dough on the hot surface, perhaps by inverting a clay pot over the dough. This imagined first oven created an environment in which the fermentation gases could be sealed within a crust of sugary starch developed by the captured heat.

From that moment, as early as six thousand years ago, it was a short step to the primitive ovens that worked on much the same principle as the expensive, high-tech gas or electric hearth ovens most artisan bakers use today. The ancestors of these modern ovens however, are the direct-fired brick or masonry ovens that are still being built today. They work like this: A space is enclosed by a floor, walls, and a roof, usually a masonry vault. A fire is built on the floor of the oven. Air to feed the fire enters through the single-front opening, which also exhausts the smoke, leaving most of the heat to collect in the masonry. Once the oven has been heated, the ashes are swept out and the formed loaves are placed directly on the floor, or hearth. The opening is closed, and residual heat radiating evenly from all surfaces of the oven, together with natural convection, bakes the bread. Because the oven is sealed, the moisture that escapes from the dough when it is heated is trapped. The captured moisture softens the skin on the formed loaf, allowing for that last burst of leavening bakers call oven spring. Because moisture conducts heat, it focuses the most intense heat on the wet surface of the loaf. This initiates a brief but complex chemical process of gelatinization and caramelization of the sugars released from the starch, which results in the rich golden sheen and sweet nutty taste of a hearth-baked loaf. The European gas or electric hearth ovens being used by many artisan bakers have been engineered to mimic this process.

The 1902 wood-fired oven at the Black Diamond Bakery in Black Diamond, Washington, still serves the community and draws travelers headed to Mount Rainier or White Pass. Not too far distant, the Ohop Valley Bakery, in Eatonville, on the southern route to Mount Rainier, produces 50 to 60 loaves a day from a wood-fired hearth oven designed and built by California ovencrafter Alan Scott in 1995. An impressive indirect-fired oven is the centerpiece of the bakery/bistro Ecco il Pane, in Vancouver, British Columbia. Smaller ovens can be found in restaurants like Seattle's Cafe Lago and many smaller bakeries throughout the Northwest.

Desserts

Cappuccino Bread Pudding with Caramel Sauce

Serves 8

After coping with a preponderance of gray skies and soggy days, many Northwesterners need their spirits lifted. Often that boost comes in the form of coffee. Here's a wonderful bread pudding from Grand Central Bakery, flavored with the Northwest's favorite pick-me-up.

½ cup espresso or 1 cup strong coffee
½ cup plus 2 tablespoons sugar
4 large eggs
4 large egg yolks
3 cups half-and-half
½ teaspoon vanilla extract
½ cup slivered almonds
5 cups trimmed and cubed (1 inch) day-old challah, brioche,
    or country white bread
1 tablespoon unsalted butter, cut into small pieces
Caramel Sauce (recipe follows)
Lightly sweetened whipped cream
Chocolate-covered espresso beans (optional)

Preheat the oven to 325°F. Grease an 8-inch-square baking dish.

Combine the espresso or coffee and 2 tablespoons sugar in a small saucepan. Bring to a boil and simmer until the liquid has reduced to ¼ cup, 3 to 4 minutes for espresso, 6 to 7 minutes for coffee. Let cool.

Whisk together the eggs, egg yolks, and ½ cup sugar in a large bowl. Whisk in the half-and-half, vanilla, and cooled espresso mixture.

Toast the almonds in a small skillet over medium heat, stirring frequently, until golden, 6 to 8 minutes. Transfer to a bowl.

Spread the bread in the baking dish and sprinkle with the almonds. Pour the egg mixture over the bread. Push the bread lightly into the liquid so it is immersed, and dot with the butter.

Place the baking dish in a larger roasting pan and fill the pan with hot water halfway up the baking dish. Bake for 1 hour and 15 minutes, or until a knife inserted in the middle comes out clean.

Serve the bread pudding warm or at room temperature with warm Caramel Sauce. Top with whipped cream and chocolate-covered espresso beans, if desired.

Caramel Sauce

Makes about 1 cup

½ cup sugar
¼ cup water
¾ cup heavy cream
Pinch of salt
2 tablespoons unsalted butter

Combine the sugar and water in a small heavy-bottomed saucepan over high heat. Bring to a boil and boil, without stirring, but swirling the contents of the pan every now and then to mix. Cook until the sugar turns a deep caramel. Remove from the heat. Pour in the cream and return to the burner. Stir until smooth and add the salt and butter. Let cool slightly.

Grand Central Summer Pudding

Serves 6 to 8

Northwest berries are absolutely astonishing. Begin the feasting in June with sweet, cultivated raspberries and strawberries. End in September with masses of blackberries, picked from the uncontrollable bushes that litter every untamed inch of soil. Any combination of these berries, coupled with an artisan bread, makes a dreamy summer pudding. And make sure you've got plenty of whipped cream.

8 slices (½-inch thick) Como or other country bread, crusts
   removed
1 pint fresh strawberries, rinsed, hulled, and cut in half
3 cups (12 ounces) fresh or frozen unsweetened raspberries
4 cups (16 ounces) fresh or frozen unsweetened blackberries
½ cup sugar
¼ cup frozen (unthawed) cranberry or orange juice concentrate
2 tablespoons orange liqueur, such as Cointreau, Grand Marnier,
   or Triple Sec (optional)
Berries, sweetened whipped cream, and fresh mint, for garnish

Preheat the oven to 400°F.

Spread the bread on a baking sheet and bake until bread is firm and dry but not toasted, 5 to 8 minutes. Arrange the bread around the sides and bottom of a 6-cup mold or bowl. Trim the bread to cover the mold completely, reserving the trimmings.

Combine the berries, sugar, juice concentrate, and liqueur in a heavy-bottomed saucepan over medium heat. Stir lightly to help the sugar dissolve while trying not to mash the berries. Ladle the fruit and liquid into the bread-lined mold. Place the reserved pieces of bread over the berries, putting the smaller pieces in the center. Place a small plate over the mold and weight it down with a large can. Refrigerate overnight or for up to 2 days before serving.

To serve, unmold onto a plate and garnish with fresh berries, whipped cream, and mint.

Fried Bread with Strawberries

Serves 4

This recipe comes from the Anjou Bakery in Cashmere, in the center of Washington State. Use a lighter bread, such as a country white, to let the flavor of the strawberries come through.

2 tablespoons unsalted butter
1 tablespoon olive oil
4 slices (¾-inch thick) artisan bread
2 tablespoons turbinado sugar (see Note) or brown sugar
1 cup sliced strawberries
¼ cup sour cream

Heat the butter and oil over medium heat in a large skillet and add as many bread slices at a time as will fit comfortably. Fry until browned on both sides, 2 to 3 minutes per side. Sprinkle with the sugar and serve warm with strawberries and dollops of sour cream.

Variation: For a savory version, sprinkle the bread with sea salt and serve with smoked salmon and cream cheese.

Note: Turbinado sugar is available at natural food stores.

Peach, Caramel, and Toasted Bread Ice Cream

Serves 4 to 6

This recipe was inspired by a very old English recipe for brown bread ice cream. In the original recipe, toasted wheat crumbs were simply added to a vanilla ice cream. Here, toasted nut bread crumbs are coated with caramel to create a candy brittle, which is broken into pieces and stirred into the ice cream. Since this recipe contains a high proportion of fruit puree, it has a very pleasing jolt of peaches, but it tends to turn a bit icy as it stands in the freezer. It's best eaten the day it's made.

3 large egg yolks
1 cup sugar
Pinch of salt
2 cups heavy cream
½ cup milk
1 teaspoon vanilla extract
6 large ripe peaches or nectarines, pitted and peeled
  (about 2 pounds)
1 cup fresh bread crumbs, made from walnut or other nut bread

Whisk together the egg yolks, ½ cup of the sugar, and salt in a large bowl until smooth. Set aside.

Combine the cream and milk in a medium saucepan and bring to a boil. Remove from the heat. Gradually whisk ½ cup of the hot cream mixture into the eggs, whisking constantly. Return the mixture to the pot and whisk well. Simmer until the cream mixture registers 170°F on a candy thermometer, or until mixture thickens and coats a spoon. Stir in the vanilla. Strain and refrigerate until cold.

Puree the peaches in a food processor until smooth. Whisk into the cooled cream and pour into an ice cream maker. Freeze according to manufacturer's instructions.

Preheat the oven to 400°F.

Spread the bread crumbs on a baking sheet and toast until browned and crisp, about 10 minutes. Set aside.

Put the remaining ½ cup sugar in a very clean small saucepan and add 2 tablespoons water. Bring to a boil, reduce the heat, and simmer, swirling (without stirring) the contents of the pan every now and then to mix, until the sugar starts to turn to a caramel. Cook until it is a rich brown color. Pour quickly over the bread crumbs. Let the mixture harden, then break into very small pieces using a food processor or mortar and pestle. When the ice cream is softly frozen, fold in the caramelized bread crumbs. Cover and freeze until ready to serve.

Baked Plum and Almond Tart

Serves 8

This rustic plum tart is a specialty of Seattle's Macrina Bakery. Filled with a batter made of bread crumbs, almonds, and plenty of butter and sugar, it's a perfect dessert to make when local plums are in.

⅓ cup plus 1 tablespoon whole almonds
2 cups fine fresh bread crumbs
2 teaspoons finely grated lemon zest
8 tablespoons (1 stick) unsalted butter, softened
1 tablespoon unsalted butter, melted
1½ cups sugar plus 1 tablespoon for sprinkling
3 large eggs
1 tablespoon vanilla extract
¼ cup heavy cream
5 to 6 small black plums or 7 prune plums, sliced ¼ inch thick
Lightly sweetened whipped cream

Preheat the oven to 375°F. Spread the almonds on a baking sheet and toast until lightly browned and fragrant, about 10 minutes. Let cool thoroughly. Finely grind the nuts in a food processor. Transfer to a medium bowl. Remove and set aside 3 tablespoons of the bread crumbs. Add the remaining bread crumbs and the lemon zest to the almonds, mix well, and set aside.

Grease a 10-inch fluted tart shell and dust heavily with the reserved 3 tablespoons of the bread crumbs.

Beat the butter with 1½ cups sugar in a large mixing bowl with an electric mixer until pale and creamy, about 5 minutes on medium speed. Add the eggs, one at a time, beating each in until incorporated. Beat in the vanilla. With a large spatula, fold in half the bread crumb mixture. Fold in half the cream, then the remaining bread crumbs and remaining cream. Pour into the tart pan and set it on a baking sheet. Arrange the plums in concentric circles and brush with the melted butter. Sprinkle with the remaining sugar. Bake at 375°F for 45 to 50 minutes, or until well browned and set. Serve warm with whipped cream.

Sources for Artisan Bread

A La Française
725 South Fidalgo Street
Seattle, WA 98108
(206) 767-1818
Wholesale location; retail locations in Pioneer
Square and University Village

Anjou Bakery
3898 Old Monitor Road
Cashmere, WA 98815
(509) 782-4360
Wholesale and retail location

Antonino Bakery, Ltd.
2142 West Fourth Avenue
Vancouver, BC V6K 1N7 Canada
(604) 733-4242
Wholesale and retail location

Ballard Baking Co.
5909 24th Avenue NW
Seattle, WA 98107
(206) 781-0091
Wholesale and retail location

Black Bear Bakery
(a division of Grand Central Baking Co.)
4834 Division Street
Portland, OR 97206
(206) 236-0136
Wholesale only

Ecco il Pane
2563 West Broadway
Vancouver, BC V6K 2E9 Canada
(604) 739-1314
Retail location

Harbor Bread Company
8812 North Harborview Drive
Gig Harbor, WA 98335
(253) 851-4181
Wholesale and retail location

Grand Central Bakery, Inc.
214 First Avenue South
Seattle, WA 98104
(206) 622-3644
(206) 768-0320 (wholesale only)
Wholesale and retail location

Grand Central Baking Co.
2230 SE Hawthorne Boulevard
Portland, OR 97214
(503) 232-0575
Wholesale and retail; additional retail locations in
Multnomah Village and at 1440 SE Widler

Holly B's Bakery
Lopez Village
Lopez Island, WA 98261
(360) 468-2133
Retail location

La Baguette et L'Echalote
1680 Johnson Street, Granville Island
Vancouver, BC V6H 3S2 Canada
(604) 684-1351
Wholesale and retail location

La Panzanella
1314 East Union
Seattle, WA 98122
(206) 325-5217
(206) 325-2090 (wholesale only)
Wholesale and retail location

La Vie en Rose
418 Commercial Avenue
Anacortes, WA 98221
(360) 299-9546
Wholesale and retail location

Le Panier Very French Bakery
1902 Pike Place
Seattle, WA 98101
(206) 441-3669
Wholesale and retail location

London's Bakehouse
10640 Main Street
Bellevue, WA 98040
(425) 688-8332
Wholesale and retail location

Macrina Bakery and Cafe
2408 First Avenue
Seattle, WA 98121
(206) 448-4032
Wholesale and retail location

Marsee Baking
1323 NW 23rd Avenue
Portland, OR 97210
(503) 295-5900
Retail; multiple locations in the Portland area

Ohop Valley Bakery
216 Washington Avenue North
Eatonville, WA 98328
(360) 832-7795
Retail location

Pavé Specialty Bakery
2613 Colby Avenue
Everett, WA 98201
(425) 252-0250
Wholesale and retail location

Pearl Bakery
102 NW Ninth Avenue
Portland, OR 97209
(503) 827-0910
Wholesale and retail location

Terra Breads
2380 West Fourth Avenue
Vancouver, BC V6K 1P1 Canada
(604) 736-1838
Wholesale and retail location; also in the public
market on Granville Island

The Avenue Bread Company
1313 Railroad Avenue
Bellingham, WA 98225
(360) 676-9274
Wholesale and retail location

The Crusty Loaf
2123 Queen Anne Avenue North
Seattle, WA 98109
(206) 282-LOAF
Retail location

The Essential Baking Co.
454 North 34th Street
Seattle, WA 98103
(206) 545-3804
Wholesale only

The Village Baker
10644 Rhody Drive
Port Hadlock, WA 98339
(360) 379-5310
Wholesale and retail location

Index